The American History Series

Gary R. Hess
BOWLING GREEN STATE UNIVERSITY

The United States at War, 1941–1945

THIRD EDITION

HARLAN DAVIDSON, INC.
WHEELING, ILLINOIS 60090

Library of Congress Cataloging-in-Publication Data

Hess, Gary R.
  The United States at war, 1941–1945 / Gary R. Hess. — 3rd ed.
    p. cm. — (The American history series)
  Includes bibliographical references and index.
  ISBN 978-0-88295-281-9
  1. World War, 1939–1945 — United States. 2. United States—History—
1933–1945. I. Title.
  D769.H47 2011
  940.53'73—dc22

                                                      2011004778

Cover: USS *Bunker Hill* hit by two Kamikazes within 30 seconds off Kyushu.
May 11, 1945. Dead-372. Wounded-264. *(80-G-323712)*

Manufactured in the United States of America
15 14 13 12 11   1 2 3 4 5 VP

To the memory of Gregory Spanos

CONTENTS

PREFACE TO THE THIRD EDITION

World War II was the most momentous event of the twentieth century, and remains one of unsurpassed popular interest. It is difficult to comprehend the extent of the conflict, death, and destruction that much of the world endured. Unlike later wars in Korea, Vietnam, and the Middle East, World War II had a clear purpose that united the public. America and its allies were fighting fascist militarism, totalitarianism, and imperialism. The goal was "unconditional surrender"—thorough defeat of Germany, Japan, Italy, and the lesser Axis powers.

The war remains a topic of compelling interest. A large portion of the History Channel programs focus on World War II, courses on the war are popular at colleges and universities, and books on the war are prominently displayed on bookstore shelves. During the last decade, a number of important books have added to an already overwhelming body of scholarship. These recent books include major studies on the decisions that led to war, the Soviet Union's wartime army, the battle of Stalingrad, combat operations in the Mediterranean, the naval war on the Atlantic Ocean, the extent of the Holocaust, the end of the war in the Pacific, and the biographies of wartime leaders, including three on Winston Chruchill.

The many stories—ranging from the scholarship of historians to the reflections of men and women who experienced the war—remind us that World War II continues to generate diverse "memories." It is remembered differently by each of the nations that sent their armies into combat. As in all wars, victors and vanquished tend to cast histories of the conflict within nationalistic frameworks, glorifying or rationalizing the outcome.

Two news stories in the last month of 2010 underlined the different ways that Americans and Japanese remember two of the monumental events of the war that their nations waged nearly seventy years ago. The stories centered on two Pacific Ocean islands—Oahu, the home of Pearl Harbor, in the Hawaiian chain and Iwo Jima, a tiny Japanese island a few hundred miles from the main Japanese islands.

On December 7 came a sobering yet reassuring report of the annual commemoration of the event that plunged the United States into war: Japan's attack on the U.S. Naval base at Pearl Harbor in Hawaii in 1941. "Remember Pearl Harbor" spurred American patriotism during the war and the "sneak attack" has always been a vital part of the American memory of the war. The 2010 ceremony, however, noted the approaching end of the "Pearl Harbor generation." Of the 84,000 servicemen stationed at Pearl Harbor and neighboring bases in December 1941, only 3,000 survive, men now in or approaching their nineties. The infirmities of old age limited the number of survivors who participated in the 69th anniversary commemoration to about 120, many of them in wheelchairs. When asked about his feelings, a ninety-three-year-old veteran, now blind, remarked: "Most important I was there in the original cast and here I am again." Indeed the dwindling numbers of veterans led the Pearl Harbor Survivors Association, which has been prominent in planning the anniversaries since its founding in 1958, to consider disbanding, but those who made it to Pearl Harbor were adamant that the group continue at least until the seventieth anniversary in 2011. One eighty-eight-year-old member said: "We're not ready to throw in the towel. Some of these old duffers, if you tried to do away with this organization, you'd have them all to fight." Balancing the inevitable demise of the Pearl Harbor survivors, the 2010 commemoration marked the dedication of a new $56 million Pearl Harbor Visitors Center and Museum. The center features indoor and outdoor galleries, interactive exhibits, two movie theaters, an amphitheater, and an education center. "We might not be able to cut the mustard any more," remarked one ninety-year-old survivor, "but this [center] assures that we won't be forgotten."

Then, just a week later, came a story from the remote Japanese island of Iwo Jima. The scene in February 1945 of the next-to-last major battle of the war in the Pacific and one of its bloodiest, Iwo Jima has been largely ignored by the Japanese and untouched for sixty-five years, uninhabited except for a small Japanese military outpost. Also forgotten by the Japanese were the nearly 22,000 of their countrymen killed in a futile effort to repel the American invaders. Over the years, however, the battle of Iwo Jima remained important to American memory, partly because it was the source of one of the war's most enduring images—the photograph of embattled marines hoisting the American flag atop Mount Suribachi, which in turn inspired a large bronze statue outside Washington D.C. That the Japanese largely forgot a bitter defeat and Americans remembered a heroic victory was not unusual.

Remarkably, at this late date, that has begun to change. Clint Eastwood's widely acclaimed 2006 film *Letters from Iwo Jima*, which presented the battle from the perspective of the Japanese soldiers, was very popular in Japan. Eschewing conventional American stereotypes of Japanese soldiers as fanatical and cruel, Eastwood provided an empathetic interpretation of the Japanese commander and his men, whose fighting blended the warrior tradition and often extraordinary bravery with fatalism, humanity, and respect for their adversary. The movie essentially introduced younger generations of Japanese to a neglected part of their country's history. The interest generated by *Letters from Iwo Jima* led the Japanese government to establish a special mission to the island which, assisted by U.S. agencies, began a painstaking search for the remains of some 12,000 unaccounted-for Japanese dead. In October 2010 the mission uncovered two mass graves that may hold the remains of as many as 2,000 Japanese soldiers. On December 15, prime minister Naoto Kan and other officials visited Iwo Jima and offered prayers at the mass graves, where they vowed to find the remains of the other casualties of the bloody battle. The first visit of a Japanese premier to Iwo Jima and the government's commitment to recovering the dead mean that a long-forgotten battle finally has entered the Japanese collective memory of the war.

The purpose of this brief volume is to recapture an important time in American history. Events were of staggering proportion: the mobilization of the United States; the months of American defeats in Asia and Europe following the Japanese attack of December 7, 1941; the assertion of Allied power in both Europe and Asia; the large battles involving nations in all-out warfare; the hope of peoples throughout the world that the conflict would lead to enduring peace; the beginning of the atomic era, dramatized by the U.S. decision to use nuclear weapons against Japan; the horrors of the Holocaust, the fullest expression of Hitler's tyranny. Such events need to be remembered. The cooperation between the United States and the Soviet Union during World War II is especially noteworthy. The Russian people and their army made significant contributions in the Allies' defeat of Germany.

The third edition of this book broadens the coverage of a few events, such as the Bataan Death March and the Battle of the Bulge, that were greatly important to Americans at the time. It also calls attention to the spectacular growth of the U.S. military, including the first women's units.

Most significantly, this volume delves more deeply into the war's moral dimension, especially ways the policy and actions of the principal Allied powers seemed inconsistent with the idealism of their cause. In the earlier editions, the debate over the use of the atomic bomb against Japan was the only moral issue discussed in detail, although questions were raised about the "collaborating with collaborators" that was part of the Anglo-American invasion of North Africa in 1942, the "strange alliance" of Western democracies with the totalitarian Soviet Union, and the saturation bombings of German and Japanese cities. In this edition, I have expanded the discussion of whether the United States could have used its power to limit the extent of the Holocaust by adopting a more liberal refugee policy or bombing the railroad lines that carried thousands of Jews and other victims to the death camps. In addition, this edition explores two other moral aspects of the war that were not treated earlier. Both are the result, in large part, of impressive books published within the last year. First, Timothy Snyder's *Bloodlands:*

Europe between Hitler and Stalin details the devastating warfare that both Germany and the Soviet Union waged against the peoples caught between them, 14 million of whom were killed by German or Soviet invaders. Snyder provides a powerful reminder of the extent to which, in this important battleground, the brutality of an Allied power was indistinguishable from that of an Axis power. Second, Madhusree Mukerjee's *Churchill's Secret War: The British Empire and the Ravaging of India During World War II* illustrates how Winston Churchill's imperial mentality led to suppression of a people seeking independence and indifference to a mass famine that claimed 3 million Indian lives.

To point to these Allied shortcomings is *not* to suggest a moral equivalency between the Axis powers and the Allies; the barbarism of Germany and Japan and their treatment of subject peoples leaves no doubt about which side had the higher moral purpose. The Allied demand for "unconditional surrender" wisely meant no compromising with genuinely evil enemies. Yet if the Allies are appropriately remembered for waging the "good war," it is also worth noting that no nation waged a "perfect war."

I am indebted to several persons. For the first edition of this book, the late series editors A. S. Eisenstadt and John Hope Franklin, offered valuable advice, as did my colleagues Bill Rock and Pat Alston. The late Harlan Davidson, a friend for many years, was supportive from our first conversations on this project. Maureen Gilgore Hewitt, formerly the editor-in-chief at Harlan Davidson, Inc., vastly improved the final manuscript of the first edition. In preparing the second edition, I benefited from the suggestions of long-time friends Bernie Sternsher and Roger Daniels as well as from the assistance of Jack Benge and Stephanie McConnell, especially in clarifying a number of matters and in updating the bibliography; Dwayne Beggs provided similar valuable help on this edition. The publisher Andrew J. Davidson encouraged and facilitated the second edition and personally edited this one. He offered a number of valuable suggestions.

Lastly, this book is dedicated to an inspiring teacher, Gregory Spanos, who in his high school history classes strongly influenced my decision to become a historian. I can recall many moments in his classes, but none more vividly than the day when his discussion on the Pearl Harbor attack abruptly shifted to a first-person narrative based on his recollections as a young soldier in Honolulu that morning. I regret very much that I never had the opportunity to tell him that this book would be dedicated to him, for he died unexpectedly shortly before the first edition of the book was published.

Gary R. Hess
Bowling Green, Ohio

CHAPTER ONE

To Pearl Harbor: The United States and World Crisis

December 7, 1941, was an uncommonly beautiful Sunday morning in Hawaii. The island of Oahu, with its lush green fields, sandy beaches, and white highway climbing above sleepy Honolulu into the hills, lay bathed in sunlight. American military personnel went leisurely about their tasks. About one-third of naval crews had weekend shore leave. Antiaircraft installations were only partly manned, and no special air reconnaissance guarded the Pearl Harbor naval base. Aboard the ships moored at Pearl Harbor, sailors were sleeping, eating, lounging on decks; in the distance they could hear the comforting sound of church bells ringing. No one realized that the time had come for war.

Just after 7:00 A.M. a radar operator picked up an enormous flight of planes approaching Oahu, but a lieutenant told monitoring personnel not to worry—the aircraft had to be American bombers arriving from the mainland. The planes were actually nearly two hundred Japanese bombers and fighters, which had taken off at dawn from carriers some 275 miles north of the Hawaiian Islands, on a mission to attack the U.S. Pacific fleet at Pearl Harbor. By 7:30, the Japanese pilots could make out in the distance Pearl Harbor and their principal targets: seventy combat ships, including eight battleships anchored along "Battleship Row."

1

At 7:55 A.M. the serenity of Pearl Harbor shattered: planes darkened the sky and the air reverberated with deafening explosions. Bombs rained down upon the fleet even as torpedoes launched from bombers tore into the hulls of battleships. Dive bombers swooped down on nearby airfields, immobilizing the grounded aircraft. The surprise was total. The Americans could offer no effective resistance.

The bodies of burned and bleeding men—some of them dead, others writhing and screaming in agony—covered the decks of ships. Under a torrent of bombs, the battleship *Arizona* burst into flames and exploded; as it sank, 1,100 men burned to death or drowned. All of the other battleships were badly damaged. As American crewmen scrambled overboard to escape, Japanese pilots mercilessly strafed them with machine gun bullets. Blazing oil sent fingers of smoke towering into the sky.

For two hours the Japanese attacked relentlessly, bombing and gunning ships, docks, airfields, and barracks. The American Pacific fleet was decimated. Casualties were staggering: 2,343 dead; 1,272 injured; 876 missing.

Just after the raid began, officials in Washington, D.C., received the message: AIR RAID PEARL HARBOR. THIS IS NO DRILL. An incredulous cabinet member reacted: "My God! This can't be true!" The American public learned of the attack when radio broadcasts were interrupted by the terse announcement: PEARL HARBOR ATTACKED BY JAPAN. Americans reacted with indignation and determination. The following day President Franklin D. Roosevelt, in a stirring message to Congress, hailed December 7 as "a date which will live in infamy." Congress, with just one dissenting vote, immediately declared war on Japan.

For the next four years Americans waged a war in which national pride lay at stake to a degree unparalleled in the American experience. Unlike responses to earlier and subsequent conflicts, no one questioned the need to fight the Axis powers. The slogan "Remember Pearl Harbor" united the American public. Not only had Japan attacked American territory, but it and its Axis partners—Nazi Germany under Adolf Hitler and fascist Italy under Benito Mussolini—threatened the fundamental traditions and values of Western civilization. For the American nation, the war constituted the price of freedom.

Prior to the Pearl Harbor attack, the American public and its leaders had been divided over how the United States should respond to the worsening world crisis. War had begun in Asia in 1937 and in Europe in 1939, but until Pearl Harbor the United States had avoided direct intervention. The nation had not, however, remained neutral, for American power and influence, under Roosevelt's leadership, was already being exerted against the Axis.

The Arsenal of Democracy: The War in Europe

The United States had greater economic, political, and cultural ties with Europe than with Asia. Although war eventually came to America in the Pacific, the nation's attention prior to Pearl Harbor focused on the crisis in Europe.

The rise of Nazi Germany under Hitler's leadership challenged the political settlement reached at the Paris Peace Conference following World War I. Initially, Britain and France had attempted to accommodate Hitler; their policy of appeasement led to the agreements reached at Munich in 1938 in which German demands for control over part of Czechoslovakia were accepted in return for Hitler's assurances that Germany would seek no more territory. When German troops seized control of the remainder of Czechoslovakia six months later, the British and the French decided that they had to resist any further advance. On September 1, 1939, that advance came—Germany invaded Poland. Two days later Britain and France declared war, beginning World War II in Europe.

Hitler assumed that the British and French, who had not resisted his takeover of Czechoslovakia, and before that Austria, would not fight for Poland. Further, he had taken precautions to eliminate the possibility that the attack on Poland might lead the Soviet Union—the successor to the Russian Empire against which Germany had fought in World War I—to come to Poland's defense. To gain such security, a week before the invasion Germany entered into a Non-Aggression Pact with the Soviet Union that gave each nation territorial gains in Eastern Europe. In any event, Britain and France were ill-prepared to help Poland, and within a few weeks German forces overran it.

While the vast majority of Americans abhorred German aggression, they did not consider Germany a threat. France, with reputedly the strongest army in the world and a seemingly impregnable system of fortification in its Maginot Line, and Great Britain, with its preponderance of naval power and the resources of its vast empire, seemingly protected the United States. Moreover, despite the rapidity of the German victory in Poland, it was widely expected that this war would be a repetition of World War I, in which the superiority of defensive weapons had frustrated offensive operations, resulting in prolonged trench warfare.

That expectation was shattered in the spring of 1940 when Germany launched a massive attack on Western Europe. Making effective use of coordinated air power and armored divisions, Germany's *Blitzkrieg* (lightning war) advanced through the Netherlands and Belgium, broke through French lines of defense, and isolated a large British army that had been sent to help defend France. Miraculously, some 350,000 British and French troops managed to escape the European continent, leaving behind a badly demoralized French people. The Germans defeated their army in less than forty days—the result of a revolution in warfare for which the French had not been prepared. It became obvious that World War II would be fought on a far larger and more urgent scale than had World War I.

As the resistance to the Germans crumbled, many voices in France called for surrender. Premier Paul Reynaud yielded power to Marshal Henri Pétain, the World War I hero who now favored ending the war. Pétain accepted Hitler's terms for an armistice on June 22, taking France out of the war and leaving Britain alone to continue the struggle. Under the armistice, the Germans occupied most of France but the southern one-third of the country and France's overseas colonies were administered by a collaborationist French government with its capital at Vichy. Pétain headed that government.

Germany's unexpected victory changed the war. The German army now stood at the English Channel prepared to launch "Operation Sea Lion"—the plan to invade Great Britain. In July 1940 the *Luftwaffe* (the German air force) began bombing British ships, ports, airfields, and cities, and waging a "terror offensive" of daytime and nighttime bombing attacks on London. The objectives were to gain control of British airspace as a prelude to an invasion, to disrupt communications, transportation, and manufacturing, and to frighten and demoralize the public. This marked the beginning of the Battle of Britain, as the Royal Air Force, which was better prepared than commonly assumed at the time, challenged the Luftwaffe and gradually prevented its dominance of the air. Meanwhile, German submarines attacked British shipping.

For the United States, the fall of France triggered a vigorous national debate over whether the war threatened its own security. In the press, on the radio, in the halls of Congress, and in other forums, internationalists and isolationists advocated sharply different policies. Internationalists, represented by the Committee to Defend America By Aiding the Allies, called for U.S. intervention to protect Britain from Hitler's power and ambitions. A group of isolationists, called America First, insisted that the United States should act only to preserve the security of the Western Hemisphere. Assistance to England, they warned, would eventually lead the nation to war. They stressed that history was repeating itself—a quarter of a century earlier the United States had been drawn unwillingly into World War I. Internationalists countered with the assertion that by assuring the survival of Britain, the United States would guarantee its own security and avoid war.

Convinced that American security depended on the defeat of Germany, President Roosevelt provided strong internationalist leadership. Through speeches and radio broadcasts, including the famed "Fireside Chats," he managed to convince the majority of Americans of the necessary risk involved in protecting Britain. Public opinion polls, beginning after the fall of France and continuing for the next year and a half, indicated that Americans regarded "defeating Hitler" as more important than "avoiding war."

American military power lay hobbled by the effects of two decades of low defense spending—largely the work of isolationists in Congress. While Roosevelt had increased the strength of the navy during his administration, the army remained pitifully weak. In 1940 it ranked eighteenth in the world. The contrast with the Axis powers was stark: while Germany had 136 divisions, the United

States could mobilize only five fully equipped ones. For that reason, Roosevelt found himself at odds with military leaders who wanted to concentrate on building the U.S. Army's strength instead of using precious resources to defend Britain.

Nevertheless, as the British and the Germans fought on the sea and in the air, Roosevelt took a series of steps to provide critical assistance to Britain. In September 1940 the president, through an executive agreement, provided the British with fifty destroyers in exchange for bases on British territories in the Western Hemisphere. The British badly needed the destroyers for the protection of merchant shipping. Roosevelt justified his unusual measure, clearly an abandonment of any pretext of neutrality, as "the most important action in the reinforcement of our national defense . . . since the Louisiana Purchase." Though outraged, isolationists were powerless to prevent the "destroyer-bases" deal.

After Roosevelt was elected president for an unprecedented third term in November 1940, he responded to urgent requests from British prime minister Winston Churchill for greater assistance; the result was the proposed Lend-Lease bill that gave the president the power to "sell, transfer title to, exchange, lease, lend, or otherwise dispose of [any defense article] to the government of any country whose defense the President deems vital to the defense of the United States." To justify this extraordinary measure, Roosevelt told the American public that the survival of England depended on arms and supplies from the United States, which had to become the "arsenal of democracy." Further outraged, isolationists charged, in the words of Senator Robert Taft (R-OH), that the measure gave the president "a blank check . . . to wage undeclared war all over the world . . . through every means except putting soldiers in the field." Taft was correct, but most Americans accepted the necessity and risks of Lend-Lease. In March 1941 both houses of Congress approved the Lend-Lease Act by substantial majorities, giving Roosevelt virtually unlimited authority to use American resources against aggressive powers.

Besides providing material support to Britain, Roosevelt took the extraordinary step of committing the United States to war aims even though the nation was not officially at war. In August 1941, he and Churchill met secretly aboard warships off the coast of Newfoundland. At the end of this first meeting of the two leaders, they issued the Atlantic Charter, which committed both nations to the "final destruction of Nazi tyranny" and to the building of a postwar world peace based on the principles of self-determination of peoples, free trade and the sharing of resources, and international cooperation to ensure security. The Atlantic Charter constituted a virtual Anglo-American alliance.

Even as Roosevelt boldly asserted the stirring idealism of the Atlantic Charter, his leadership faced a strong challenge from the isolationists as Congress debated "extending" the Selective Service Act of 1940. That legislation (the first peacetime draft in American history) had obligated draftees for a one-year tour of duty, but in 1941 the army leadership looked upon their impending discharges as catastrophic to national defense. In response, Roosevelt supported legislation to extend the tours of duty for another eighteen months. In emotional rhetoric, congressional critics charged "a breach of contract" with the draftees. It took all of the Roosevelt administration's efforts to overcome isolationist opposition. In the end, the measure won approval by a vote of 45 to 30 in the Senate and by the razor-thin margin of one vote—203 to 202—in the House of Representatives. The contrast between the internationalist commitment of the Atlantic Charter and the narrow victory over isolationists in Congress was striking. "The Americans are a curious people," an Englishman observed, "I can't make them out. One day they're announcing they'll guarantee freedom and fair play for everybody in the world. The next day they are deciding by one vote that they'll go on having an army."

By the fall of 1941, the commitment to Britain led the United States into undeclared naval warfare in the North Atlantic. As a consequence of German submarine attacks that took a heavy toll on ships headed for the British Isles, the U.S. Navy, at Roosevelt's order, began escorting British convoys carrying supplies across the Atlantic with authorization to "shoot on sight" any enemy ships. Inevitably, American and German vessels clashed, and lives were lost. In mid-October, a German submarine torpedoed the U.S. destroyer, *Kearney*, killing eleven Americans; Roosevelt told the nation, "We have wished to avoid shooting. But the shooting has started. And history has recorded who fired the first shot." A few days later, on

October 31, a more devastating submarine attack, this one on the destroyer *Reuben James*, took 115 American lives.

By the time of the Atlantic Charter and the beginning of naval warfare, the conflict in Europe had broadened. On June 22, 1941, Germany disregarded the Non-Aggression Pact and invaded the Soviet Union. Most observers anticipated that the Russians would be unable to withstand the German offensive; indeed, in the early weeks of the Russian campaign, German forces encountered little resistance. By late summer the Russian army slowed the German advance. Britain and the United States decided that their interests necessitated helping the Soviets survive. Putting aside their aversion to communism and their resentment over the Non-Aggression Pact of 1939, the British and Americans provided assistance to the beleaguered Soviets. (Churchill commented "If Hitler invaded Hell, I would make at least a favorable reference to the Devil in the House of Commons.") Ignoring domestic critics, Roosevelt in late October authorized Lend-Lease assistance to the Soviet Union.

While Americans generally supported Roosevelt's initiatives, public opinion as measured by opinion polls and editorial comment in the press overwhelmingly opposed military intervention. Even the loss of American lives in the naval warfare of late 1941 failed to arouse the kind of public indignation that had helped send the United States to war under similar circumstances in 1898 and in 1917. A majority of Americans believed that Germany could be defeated without U.S. military intervention. By late 1941 the survival of England and the hope that the Russians could withstand the German invasion lent support to public expectations that being the "arsenal of democracy" might be the uppermost limit of American involvement. Japan's decision for war shattered that hope.

"Not Enough Ships": The Effort to Restrain Japan

While the crisis in Europe preoccupied Americans, they also faced the threat of Japanese expansion in Asia. Since the late nineteenth century, Japan and the United States had been rivals in the Pacific. Both nations had emerged as major powers during the late nineteenth century, with interests in political and economic expansion in Asia.

In each case, military victories signaled regional influence. For the United States, easy conquests in the Spanish-American War of 1898 brought control of former Spanish possessions in Asia—the Philippine Islands and the island of Guam. In the course of that conflict, the United States also annexed the Hawaiian Islands. The Japanese defeat of China in the 1894–95 Sino-Japanese War demonstrated Japan's strength and gave the victors important concessions, including control of the island of Taiwan and predominance in parts of the Chinese province of Manchuria, the mineral resources of which the Japanese coveted. Even more surprising was Japan's victory over Russia a decade later, in the Russo-Japanese War (1904–05), which resulted in Japanese dominance over Korea and tighter control of Manchuria.

As new powers in Asia, the United States and Japan disagreed about the status of China; each had an interest in expanding trade and investment opportunities there (as did Britain, France, and other European powers). The United States supported Chinese independence, but throughout the early decades of the twentieth century, China found itself torn by revolution, xenophobia, and factionalism—circumstances that seemingly invited foreign intervention.

After World War I, in which Japan and the United States were wary allies, the two powers had moved toward understanding and cooperation. At the Washington Conference of 1921–22, they joined with other nations with interests in East Asia and the Pacific to reach agreements to uphold China's integrity, respect one another's territorial possessions, and limit naval armaments. Japan thus became integrated economically and politically with the West, leading to an era of close relations with the United States.

The Great Depression of the 1930s, however, greatly undermined Japan's commitment to international cooperation. Domestic hardships had led all industrialized nations to protect their fragile economies. For its part, the United States enacted the highest tariff in its history, triggering a drastic reduction in world trade as other nations followed suit. Japan's leaders increasingly saw the survival of their small island nation—with limited natural resources and dependent on the importation of raw materials and the exportation of manufactured goods—threatened by a hostile world, and they came to believe that territorial expansion was vital to their national security. While all who led Japan accepted the necessity of expansion, they disagreed over tactics. Moderates, who wanted to avoid conflict, clashed with ultranationalists, who were prepared to act unilaterally and risk war to achieve expansion.

While leaders in Tokyo remained divided over the nation's course, the Japanese army under ultranationalist commanders took the initiative. In 1931, it provoked an "incident" with Chinese forces in Manchuria that became the pretext to eliminate the last vestiges of Chinese authority there. Later, in 1937, the Japanese military used another clash with the Chinese, the Marco Polo Bridge incident, to launch a large-scale invasion, which resulted in Japanese domination of large swaths of northern and coastal China. Having greatly expanded their economic holdings in Manchuria and northern China, Japan proclaimed the New Order for East Asia, a scheme of regional economic cooperation under its domination.

Japan's aggressive acts of warfare against China appalled Americans. Roosevelt attempted to arouse public sentiment on behalf of uniting with other nations to "quarantine" aggressors and provide some financial support and war materials to the Chinese, but the strength of the isolationists precluded the possibility of the United States giving any meaningful help. Still, left indelibly in the minds of Americans was the image of Japan's savagery against the Chinese. The most horrendous act was the so-called Rape of Nanking in late 1937 and early 1938—described by Iris Chang as the "forgotten Holocaust" of World War II. In their assault on the Chinese capital, the Japanese brutally massacred approximately 350,000 Chinese. Chang writes:

> When the city fell on December 13, 1937, Japanese soldiers began an orgy of cruelty seldom if ever matched in world history. Tens of thousands of young men were rounded up and herded to the outer limits of the city, where they were mowed down by machine guns, used for bayonet practice, or soaked with gasoline and burned alive. For months the streets of the city were heaped with corpses and reeked with the stench of rotting human flesh.

Forcing the Japanese to withdraw from China became an American objective, one based on the historic commitment to China's integrity and reinforced by moral indignation.

Although Japanese forces controlled large parts of China, they had not defeated the Chinese and were mired in combating continuing resistance. Moreover, Japan remained dependent on the United States for one-third of its imports, including petroleum, iron, and machine goods. The course of the war in Europe provided an opportunity for Japan to resolve its critical position. The 1940 German *blitzkrieg* signaled Japan that the time was right to expand into Southeast Asia, with its abundant resources of tin, oil, and rubber. Clearly, the European powers that dominated most of that region were no longer capable of defending their interests. The beleaguered British lacked adequate numbers of men and supplies to defend Malaya and Burma. The defeated Dutch could not protect the Netherlands East Indies (present-day Indonesia), nor could the French withstand pressures on French Indochina (Vietnam, Laos, Cambodia). Only the United States, which had its own imperial obligations to the Philippines, was left to uphold Western predominance in the region. Seeing their interests tied to German success, the Japanese, in late 1940, entered into the Tripartite Pact with Germany and Italy, establishing the Axis Alliance.

Intent on expansion into Southeast Asia, the Japanese sought assurance against an attack from their historic rival to the north—Russia. Accordingly, Foreign Minister Yosuke Matsuoka, who had led Japan into the Tripartite Pact, negotiated a mutual nonaggression pact with the Soviet Union. When Germany invaded Russia, the Japanese felt even more secure, for now the Soviet Union had to give priority to defending its European territories. At this point the Japanese cautiously planned their "southern advance," with the remainder of French Indochina as the first target.

While agreeing that the United States had to restrain Japan, U.S. officials differed over tactics. Just as the government in Tokyo was divided between ultranationalists and moderates, so the government in Washington was divided between moderates and hard-liners. The moderates—led by Secretary of State Cordell Hull, Under Secretary of State Sumner Welles, and Ambassador to Japan Joseph

Grew—believed it essential to seek points of cooperation with Japan and opposed imposing stringent pressures. Japan could be pushed, they warned, into a situation in which its leaders would see war as preferable to humiliation and retreat. Hard-liners—represented by Secretary of War Henry Stimson and Secretary of the Treasury Henry Morgenthau—discounted Japan's willingness and ability to wage war against the United States and insisted that economic pressures could force Japan to abandon its expansionist plans.

With the survival of England the overriding U.S. priority, Roosevelt wanted to avoid war in the Pacific. He told an adviser in early July 1941: "It is terribly important for the control of the Atlantic for us to keep peace in the Pacific. I simply have not got enough ships to go around—and every little episode in the Pacific means fewer ships in the Atlantic." He recognized that the Japanese themselves were divided over their future course. On another occasion, he said: "The Japanese are having a real drag-down and knock-out fight among themselves and have been . . . trying to decide which way they are going to jump—attack Russia, attack the South Seas . . . or whether they will sit on the fence and be friendly with us. No one knows what their decision will be."

When Japan ended that uncertainty by sending 40,000 troops into southern Indochina to complete its domination of the French colony, Roosevelt responded vigorously. His executive order of July 25, 1941, froze all Japanese assets in the United States, imposed an embargo on the island nation, and ended the export of petroleum to Japan. It is now evident that in issuing this order Roosevelt did not intend to cut off all such exports. He shared the concerns of moderates and simply wanted to control the *amount* of oil exported to Japan. He told advisers that he preferred one step at a time, "to slip the noose around Japan's neck, and give it a jerk every now and then." Despite the unconditional language of the July 25 announcement, the United States intended to impose a total embargo only if Japan refused to moderate its policies. Contrary to the president's intention, however, second-echelon officials in the Department of State went ahead and imposed a total embargo.

And that total embargo remained in place despite Roosevelt's intention; the reasons why were political and diplomatic. The American public strongly supported the embargo. Moreover, with the embargo already announced, U.S. officials feared that the Japanese would view any modification of the decree as a sign of American weakness.

American pressure influenced a final gesture by Japanese moderates to lessen the growing crisis. In late August, the prime minister, Prince Fumimaro Konoye, who led the faction anxious to avoid war, proposed to Roosevelt that they meet personally to resolve differences. Konoye's appeal reflected his apprehension that the U.S. embargo was playing into the hands of the ultranationalists; the time to avoid war, he knew, was running out. Only a summit conference promised an opportunity to hasten the diplomatic process. At first, the possibility of such a meeting intrigued Roosevelt. Yet the United States insisted on preconditions that Konoye could not accept, stipulating that the Japanese present a "clear-cut manifestation" of their intent to withdraw from both China and Indochina. This amounted to a demand that Japan relinquish its conquests of the previous decade and abandon plans for a New Order in Asia, which would have been disastrous to Konoye's position at home.

Roosevelt's backing away from the meeting reflected the domestic and international consequences of any appearance of compromising with Japan. As was evident in the response to the embargo, the American public had concluded, based on the experience of the Western democracies' efforts to appease Hitler, that compromise with aggressive powers was impossible, as it only encouraged them to act more belligerently. These sentiments were intensified toward Japan, both because of an extant race prejudice against Japanese Americans and immigrants by the white majority living on the West Coast as well as the strong popular sympathy for the Chinese in their struggle against their neighbors. At a time when Roosevelt was encouraging Chinese resistance, a conference with Konoye would have undermined Sino-American relations. In sum, constraints at home and overseas limited Roosevelt's maneuverablility.

With the imposition of the embargo and no relief in sight, Japanese leaders concluded that they had to take active control of their nation's destiny. As they saw it, for a decade their policy had been one of drift and uncertainty, largely dependent on external events. Historian Akira Iriye remarks that the "sense of aimlessness was numbing" among Japanese officials. The conviction that the time had come for a definite decision led to a change in Japan's leadership; in October, Prince Konoye was replaced as premier by General Hideki Tojo, a move taken to break the deadlock of indecision.

From the perspective of Japan's leaders, the actions of the United States had forced Japan's hand. As negotiations between Japanese envoys and American officials went on, it became apparent that the United States would not compromise—it sought Japan's recognition of Chinese integrity, the withdrawal of Japanese forces from China, and an abandonment of Japanese expansionism. While some Japanese leaders still wanted to avoid war with the United States, the drift of events and the sense that it was time to seize the initiative drove the decision for war. Japan, it seemed, had come too far to retreat under American pressure; national survival mandated expansion, which by late 1941 could be fulfilled only by war.

However strongly the international situation forged the logic of war, Japan's leaders recognized that the United States, with its larger population, industrial supremacy, and far greater resources, would defeat Japan in a conflict of any duration. In the conferences of Japanese officials in the fall of 1941, neither army nor navy officers predicted victory; indeed, they warned that Japan would be in serious trouble if the war lasted more than two years. Yet Japan's leaders remained undeterred. They calculated that the war would not be a prolonged one because the United States, forced to fight in both Europe and Asia, would accept a negotiated settlement with Japan in order to concentrate on liberating Europe from Nazi domination.

In anticipating this outcome, the Japanese expected history to repeat itself, for the memory of the Russo-Japanese War of 1904–05 was still prominent in the minds of the decision makers. In that conflict, Japan made use of a surprise attack before a declaration of war to gain an early military advantage over the Russians; then, as the Japanese began to lose that initiative, a mediator (ironically, the United States) had helped to end the war on terms favorable to

Japan. "One suspects that either consciously or unconsciously," the historian Nabutaka Ike has written, "the Japanese leaders in 1941 were hoping for a more or less similar sequence of events."

A critical view of such thinking might argue that the Japanese lacked realism in their assessment of the situation. There were many uncertainties in the course of events as anticipated by Tokyo: Would Germany continue to win the war in Europe? Would the Americans grow weary of fighting on two fronts? Would the Americans accept a settlement favorable to Japan? Would any third-party nation have an interest in mediating the Japanese-American differences? Those questions had negligible effect on the decision-making process, partly because a sense of fatalism prevailed among Japan's leaders. When some officers questioned the advisability of war, Admiral Isoruku Yamamoto, commander-in-chief of the fleet, responded: "The only question that remains is the blessing of Heaven. If we have Heaven's blessing, there will be no doubt of success."

Japanese leaders, convinced that unless the United States made concessions war was necessary, planned a surprise attack against the major American base in the Pacific—Pearl Harbor. The objective was to destroy the U.S. Pacific fleet, the principal deterrent to Japan's New Order. Admiral Yamamoto devised the plan for the attack. To assure surprise, negotiations were to continue with the Americans even as a large naval task force headed toward Hawaii—a distance of some 3,500 miles from Japan—without being detected.

Simultaneously with the Pearl Harbor attack, the Japanese planned to bomb American bases in the Philippine Islands, Wake Island, and Guam; these strikes were to be followed quickly by invasion of those American territories. The Japanese also expected to extend their military control over all of Southeast Asia, thereby gaining control of the area's resources. To secure the establishment of this empire, Japan would have to capture additional islands in the southern and western Pacific; those islands would provide Japan with a defensive perimeter—a shield of naval and air bases against any resurgence of American power in the region. Finally, with control of the western Pacific and Southeast Asia firmly established, the Japanese could complete the subjugation of China, which would be shut off from assistance.

This vast empire was as ambitious as any ever conceived by any nation. Japan sought to control the Asian landmass and islands stretching from Burma to the central Pacific. Japan's New Order as envisioned by the men planning war in the fall of 1941 would include fully one-half of the world's population.

The key to this monumental undertaking was the destruction of the U.S. Pacific fleet. The Japanese secretly amassed a large naval force at a remote base in the Kurile Islands, which lie to the north of the main Japanese islands. When the men who manned the ships in that force learned that their mission was to attack Pearl Harbor, they were elated; one of the seamen later reflected on his feelings at the time: "An air attack on HAWAII: A dream come true. . . . We would teach the arrogant Anglo-Saxon scoundrels a lesson!"

On November 26 the task force—six carriers with 423 planes, nine destroyers, two battleships, three cruisers, three submarines, and seven tankers—left the Kuriles and began its long advance across the northern Pacific. Preceding the task force was an advance force of twenty-seven submarines. The task force, as expected, encountered bad weather—fog and heavy seas—but because of the remoteness of the water it crossed, it avoided detection. Vice Admiral Chuichi Nagumo had orders to attack Pearl Harbor on the morning of Sunday, December 7. He understood that the mission might be aborted under one of two conditions: enemy detection of the task force or orders from Tokyo to return (which leaders would issue if the United States accepted Japan's final demands). As neither of these contingencies occurred, on December 2 Nagumo received the code signal to commence hostilities five days later.

In view of the deteriorating relations with Japan, why did the United States fail to anticipate an attack on Pearl Harbor? This question takes on special significance because, unknown to Japan, American cryptanalysts had succeeded in breaking the top-secret Japanese diplomatic code. The success of Operation MAGIC—the U.S. military's secret intercept and translation of coded messages—meant that selected American officials knew the contents of messages transmitted between the government in Tokyo and its embassies throughout the world, including Washington. In addition to MAGIC, American intelligence officers monitored radio signals from the Japanese army and navy; while those codes had not been broken, the volume and location of the messages provided much data on military concentrations and movements. Finally, the American government received information from diplomatic outposts, including its embassy in Tokyo, which provided substantial analyses of developments within Japan.

What specifically did the United States learn from this voluminous intelligence? As a result of MAGIC, it was clear that the Japanese had set a deadline for a negotiated settlement; in the absence of agreement before November 29, the Japanese informed their embassy in Washington that "things are automatically going to happen." Americans also knew that the Japanese considered a proposed basis for a settlement, delivered to Secretary Hull on November 20, to be their "last" offer. From MAGIC and other sources, U.S. officials knew with certainty that the Japanese were planning for military operations in Southeast Asia.

But if the intelligence reports signaled clear Japanese intentions, they also provided misleading information. The Japanese leadership, in order to ensure their strategy of surprise attack, took extraordinary steps to keep knowledge of the Pearl Harbor operation restricted: they never shared the plan with Japanese emissaries overseas; they, too, knew only that "things [were] automatically going to happen." The naval task force charged with attacking Pearl Harbor was dispatched in utmost secrecy, so American intelligence officials had no knowledge of its mission across the northern Pacific. The Japanese also deliberately sent out messages with much irrelevant information to suggest that Japan was either planning an attack on the Soviet Union or a major offensive in China.

Finally, available intelligence revealed neither the date nor the place of any planned aggression. American intelligence fully expected the Japanese to attack somewhere in Southeast Asia during the first or second week of December. It was assumed that the attack would occur in the Netherlands East Indies, Thailand, or Malaya. It seemed unlikely that any U.S. territory would come under attack, but, if so, the Philippines or Guam were the anticipated targets.

As a few sensational accounts of the Pearl Harbor attack have emphasized, there were, in the wealth of intelligence gathered by the United States, a few hints of Japanese interest in Pearl Harbor and a couple of rumors of plans to attack the U.S. Pacific fleet. For several reasons, however, American officials understandably discounted any suggestion of an attack on Pearl Harbor. The sources of such reports seemed to be of questionable reliability; for instance, Ambassador Grew reported in early 1941 that the Peruvian minister in Tokyo had informed him of a rumor that the Japanese were planning an attack on Pearl Harbor, but intelligence officers did not take the story seriously, especially when investigation located the source of the rumor as the minister's Japanese cook. Moreover, the overwhelming volume of evidence pointed toward aggression in Southeast Asia, and an attack in the middle of the Pacific simply seemed beyond Japan's capacity.

The principal shortcomings of the official American reaction rested in a mentality that underestimated Japan's military ability and willingness to wage war against the United States. American officials saw Japan as a second-rate power, virtually bankrupt, short of raw materials, and bogged down militarily in China. American intelligence officers and other leaders assumed that Japan would act in a manner consistent with an American definition of "rationality." This meant expanding into Southeast Asia to gain necessary resources, an action which the United States would have been powerless to prevent. "Rationality" further suggested that the Japanese would not move against the Philippines but against the European colonies on the Asian mainland. Why should the Japanese force war with the United States? To attack Pearl Harbor seemed, in the words of one military officer, "utterly stupid." As another officer later commented, Americans made the mistake of imputing to the Japanese "the highest form of good sense and good judgment." Missing from the American interpretation of Japan's intentions was an understanding of the prevailing mentality in Tokyo. Americans did not comprehend the profound Japanese sense of desperation to end paralyzing indecision over the nation's future. In short, the American view of Japan was oblivious to the factors that forced Japan's leaders to decide that their national survival necessitated war. The American assessment of the Japanese also persistently downgraded Japan's military, which for decades had been enlarged, modernized, and politicized: by 1941, a well-trained force with a professional officer corps confident that it could wage war against the United States.

So the Japanese achieved surprise with their devastating attack on Pearl Harbor, the impact of which was global. To the British and Russians, it meant that the United States would now become a full military partner in World War II. To the Japanese, it meant the elimination of U.S. naval power in the Pacific and the freedom to build their empire. To the Germans, it meant that the Americans had been badly crippled and that Japan had proved itself a worthy ally.

For a few days, however, it remained unclear whether Pearl Harbor would lead to immediate war between the United States and Germany. Hitler made that decision. On December 11, Germany declared war on the United States. Mindful of the critical importance of the United States in World War I, Hitler and other German leaders recognized the industrial and military potential of the United States and therefore had tolerated American naval warfare on the Atlantic and other forms of support of the British. Yet Hitler was also convinced that war with the United States was inevitable and had already assured the Japanese of German support in the event of Japanese-American warfare.

Later in December, representatives of the nations allied against the Axis met in Washington. Led by the United States, Great Britain, the Soviet Union, and China, the Allied Coalition of twenty-six nations signed the Declaration of the United Nations on January 1, 1942. The Allies committed themselves to fighting together against the Axis and to establishing a postwar world based on the principles of the Atlantic Charter. Thus, the United States was thrust into a global war. The American people faced, in the months and years to come, the most momentous challenge in their history.

CHAPTER TWO

Allied Defeats and the Axis Ascendancy, 1941–1942

The losses at Pearl Harbor marked the beginning of the darkest period in American military history. For the next six months the United States and its allies suffered defeats and retreated before superior Axis forces. The Axis powers controlled the greater parts of the European and Asian continents, North Africa, and the islands of the western Pacific, and they dominated the Pacific, Atlantic, and Indian oceans. Never before had Americans been so threatened and insecure as in the enemy-dominated world of the last weeks of 1941 and the early months of 1942.

The Nazi Empire at Its Peak

Germany exploited its advantage on three fronts: the Battle of the Atlantic against the British and American navies; the struggle in North Africa against the British army; and the war on the vast Eastern Front against the Soviet Union.

In waging the naval war, the German U-boat (submarine) campaign took a staggering toll on the shipping essential to the survival of England and Russia. In adadition to the U-boats, surface-raiders and the antishipping force of the Luftwaffe also attacked Allied

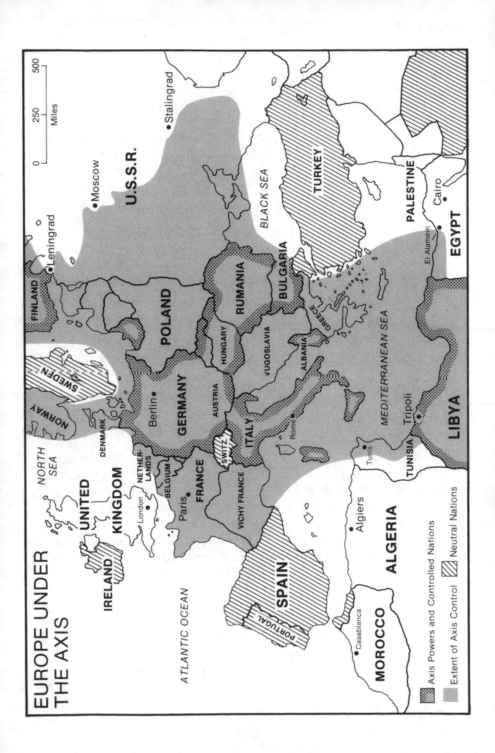

EUROPE UNDER THE AXIS

Axis Powers and Controlled Nations

Extent of Axis Control

Neutral Nations

merchant and naval ships. Still, the submarine remained the key to German success, as it accounted for more than two-thirds of Allied shipping losses.

Germany's successes in the land war worked to its advantage on the Atlantic. The capture of Norway and France in the spring of 1940 gave Germany additional bases from which its submarines could assault Allied shipping. Italy's entry into the war at that same time added to the naval strength of the Axis in the Mediterranean, facilitating Germany's ability to concentrate on the Atlantic. A year later the German invasion of the Soviet Union increased demands on the British and American navies in order to supply Russia. The most direct route—through the Barents Sea port of Murmansk—meant that British-American convoys had to cross the icy, submarine-infested waters of the North Atlantic and, after passing the Arctic Circle, proceed along the northern coast of the Scandinavian Peninsula before reaching the Soviet Union. Known in the navy as the "suicide run to Murmansk," this supply route was especially vulnerable to German attack. In one Allied convoy alone, for example, the Germans managed to sink twenty-two of thirty-three ships.

American losses in the Pacific further weakened the Allies in the Atlantic. With its Pacific fleet virtually decimated, the United States transferred part of its Atlantic fleet to the Pacific. In addition, many of the new ships being constructed in the United States were assigned to the Pacific. This reduction of American strength in the Atlantic emboldened the Germans, who no longer restricted U-boat activity to the eastern half of the Atlantic but ranged across the ocean and aimed their attacks at ships near the American coast. The German capacity to carry out such extensive naval warfare resulted from an impressive build up of its U-boat fleet. At the beginning of the European war in September 1939, the Germans had just fifty-six submarines, but by January 1942 the U-boat fleet totaled 250.

For the Allies, the Battle of the Atlantic went disastrously. Between September 1939 and December 1941, the Germans sank 8 million tons of Allied merchant shipping—heavy losses under any circumstances. Yet during the next six months, the strengthened German navy intensified its assaults and took a staggering toll of 4.5 million tons. Every four hours an Allied ship and crew were lost.

British and American shipyards working around the clock could not produce sufficient ships to keep pace with the losses. Moreover, the strength of the German navy not only disrupted the shipment of vital supplies to Britain and Russia, but it also precluded large-scale transport of troops who had to reach Europe if the Allies were going to reverse Axis control of the continent. To many observers it seemed that the Allies had lost the Battle of the Atlantic. British Prime Minister Winston Churchill wrote later that the Battle of the Atlantic was "the only thing that ever really frightened me during the war."

On the Eastern Front, German armies remained deep in Russian territory. The long front stretched from the Baltic Sea in the north to the Black Sea in the south. While the invasion had encountered greater resistance than Hitler anticipated, German armies controlled most of western Russia. A Russian counteroffensive reduced some of the pressure on Moscow. The winter of 1941–42 led to a lull in the fighting, but behind the lines the Russian people suffered from shortages of food, fuel, and clothing.

Germany launched a large offensive in May 1942. Its objective was the capture of the strategically important Caucasus in southern Russia, which, once secured, would provide needed oil and food grains. The Germans advanced quickly, leading many observers in the United States and England to doubt whether the Soviet army could offer effective resistance. Russian morale, which had broken in the face of the German invasion during World War I, likewise seemed fragile. Altogether, then, the Allied position on the Eastern Front—to which Hitler had committed the greater part of his re-sources—remained precarious.

In North Africa, the Axis forces regained the initiative early in 1942 and again threatened to capture Egypt and the Suez Canal. After having been pushed into Libya by the British in late 1941, the Axis quickly recovered, owing to the Italian navy's control of the Mediterranean and Hitler's movement of additional air support dur-ing the winter lull on the Eastern Front. The reinforced Axis seized the initiative. General Erwin Rommel, the "Desert Fox," caught the British by surprise with an advance across eastern Libya in late May; its objective was Tobruk, the strategic Mediterranean port near the

Libyan-Egyptian border. With Tobruk's fall on June 20, the Axis conquest of Egypt and the Suez Canal appeared imminent.

Japan's Imperial Conquests

In Asia, the Japanese, moving with almost incredible speed and efficiency, established control over a vast area. Taking advantage of the initiative gained at Pearl Harbor, Japan startled the Allies with an advance that signaled the establishment of their New Order. True to plan, the Pearl Harbor attack coincided with air raids on other American possessions—the Philippines, Guam, and Wake Island—as well as on the British colonies of Hong Kong, Malaya, and Burma, and the occupation of Thailand. Guam, site of the American naval base in the Marianas, fell quickly. On December 10 a Japanese air attack on the British fleet off Malaya resulted in the sinking of the battleship *Prince of Wales* and the battle cruiser *Repulse*—which the British had just dispatched to buttress their naval base at Singapore.

After a gallant defense, the American force on Wake Island finally yielded to Japan's superior numbers and control of the air and sea by surrendering on December 22. Three days later— Christmas Day—the British colony Hong Kong fell. Following an advance across Malaya, the Japanese in early February attacked the supposedly impregnable Singapore. On February 15, 1942, the badly outmaneuvered British force there surrendered, with the Japanese taking 80,000 prisoners. The imperial forces then pressed into Burma and advanced in the Dutch East Indies, which they controlled within a month.

Japan's imperial conquests from December 1941 to the spring of 1942 resulted from skillful planning and execution. Coordination of air and naval power facilitated the landing of troops at key points from which they advanced across much territory. Japan also benefited from the lack of preparedness on the part of the defenders of Southeast Asia. The British and Dutch, like the Americans prior to Pearl Harbor, tended to discount Japan's military power; at Singapore the indifference of British military leaders bordered on the scandalous. Neither the British nor the Dutch could rely on native troops—Malayan, Burmese, Javanese, or others—to fight at their side in the defense of their overseas empires.

The conquest of Southeast Asia fulfilled the pre–Pearl Harbor plans of the Japanese and gave them access to the natural resources of the region. At last, Tokyo had oil from the East Indies and tin and rubber from Malaya. With their navy dominating the western Pacific and much of the Indian Ocean, the Japanese had attained the superiority that they assumed would discourage the Americans from thwarting their gains. Calculating as well that the Germans would continue to win the war in Europe and that the United States would give priority to the European struggle, the Japanese anticipated a war-weary America eventually would accept a negotiated settlement in Asia.

The Japanese failed, however, to comprehend the effect of their actions of 1941–42 on the American government and public. When asked how the United States should fight in the Pacific, only 1 percent of the American people favored "withdraw and make peace" (the kind of response Japanese strategy had predicted—even counted on). Instead, the overwhelming majority of Americans (88 percent) said the United States should "fight an all-out war against Japan wherever we can possibly attack them." The attack on Pearl Harbor and the retreat of the United States from the western Pacific—in particular the loss of the Philippines—left Americans utterly determined to defeat the Japanese, regardless of the cost and sacrifice.

Defeat and Surrender in the Philippines

For the United States the most humiliating experience of the war was the loss of the Philippine Islands. An ill-prepared, outnumbered, inadequately supplied, and disease-ridden army of Americans and Filipinos resisted the Japanese invaders for six months before surrendering. The Stars and Stripes, which had flown over the Philippines since 1898, was replaced in May 1942 by the Rising Sun of Japan. This defeat and its aftermath—the Bataan Death March in which American and Philippine prisoners were subjected to barbaric treatment by their captors—left a strong impression on the American people, stirring deep emotions that only added to the American determination to defeat the Japanese.

The Philippine Islands—a vast archipelago of more than 7,000 islands, the largest of which are Luzon and Mindanao, and which

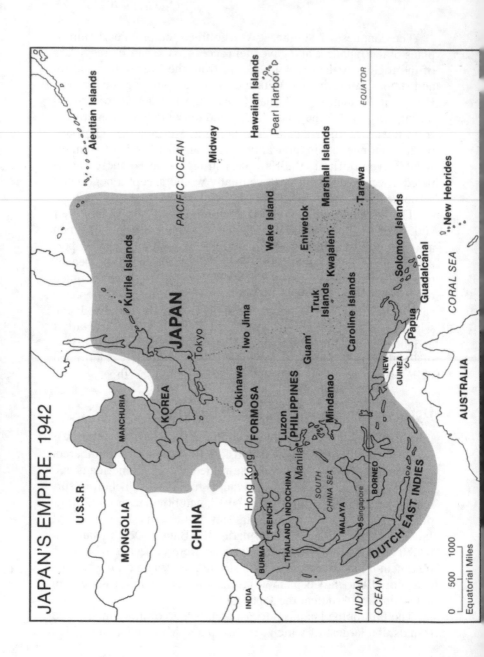

JAPAN'S EMPIRE, 1942

U.S.S.R.

MONGOLIA

MANCHURIA

CHINA

KOREA

JAPAN

Tokyo

Kurile Islands

Aleutian Islands

PACIFIC OCEAN

Midway

Hawaiian Islands

Pearl Harbor

EQUATOR

INDIA

BURMA

THAILAND

FRENCH INDOCHINA

Hong Kong

FORMOSA

Okinawa

Iwo Jima

Wake Island

Eniwetok

Marshall Islands

Tarawa

SOUTH CHINA SEA

Luzon

Manila

PHILIPPINES

Mindanao

Guam

Truk Islands

Kwajalein

Caroline Islands

Solomon Islands

New Hebrides

MALAYA

Singapore

BORNEO

DUTCH EAST INDIES

NEW GUINEA

Papua

Guadalcanal

CORAL SEA

AUSTRALIA

INDIAN OCEAN

0   500   1000
Equatorial Miles

had in 1940 a population of about 16 million—had been an American possession since the Spanish-American War. Unlike other imperial powers of the early twentieth century, the United States had fostered measures of self-government in its Asian territory; this policy culminated in the establishment in 1935 of the Philippine Commonwealth, intended as a transitional government to guide the nation to complete independence in 1946. In addition, American rule had brought improvements in education, social services, communications, and transportation. To be sure, American imperialism had its negative features, including the suppression of a nationalist rebellion at the turn of the century and commercial restrictions that discouraged diversification of the Philippine economy and created dependency on the American market. Nonetheless, American control did not breed the strong resentment often characteristic of native attitudes toward colonial powers, and the benign nature of American rule contributed to Philippine identification with the American war effort. Filipinos generally remained loyal, and thousands fought side by side with the American soldiers; the Japanese encountered greater resistance in the Philippines than in Malaya, Burma, or the Netherlands East Indies, where native peoples lacked any identification with their European rulers.

American strategists had long recognized that in the event of a war with Japan, the Philippine Islands would be virtually impossible to defend. Accordingly, in developing a contingency plan (known as War Plan Orange) for such a conflict, it had been assumed that following a Japanese invasion, reinforcements would not reach the islands for six months. During that period, American and Philippine forces were to defend two positions: the Bataan Peninsula and the island of Corregidor. By holding those points in Manila Bay on the island of Luzon, the defenders would deny the Japanese control of Manila Harbor, which was vital to control of the islands and to operations elsewhere in the region. This plan for a limited defense of the Philippines was reaffirmed as the United States in 1941 developed strategies for a global war against both Germany and Japan. Based on the concern that the major enemy would be Germany, the new War Plan Rainbow called for only minimal effort in the Pacific, including the early withdrawal from the Philippines after offering resistance in Bataan and Corregidor.

General Douglas MacArthur had long experience in the Philippines, including service as military adviser to the Commonwealth government from 1835 to July 1941, when he was recalled to active duty to become commanding general of the United States Army forces in the Far East. MacArthur advocated a buildup of the Philippine army and a commitment to defend the entire coast: rather than retreat to Bataan and Corregidor, the Americans and the Filipinos, he argued, should resist *any* Japanese landings. Owing largely to MacArthur's glowing reports about the progress of Philippine forces, his superiors in Washington authorized his broader plan to defend the archipelago.

The prospect for any effective defense of the Philippines was shattered by the events of the first day of the war. The attack on Pearl Harbor eliminated the possibility of any assistance from the Pacific fleet. And, a few hours later, the Japanese bombed Clark Field, the major U.S. air base in the Philippines. Again having caught the Americans by surprise, the Japanese found the U.S. aircraft on the ground—easy and inviting targets. This raid eliminated most of the aircraft available to defend the Philippines. Louis Morton, official historian of the campaign in the Philippines, has written: "hopes for active defense of the Islands rested on these aircraft. At the end of the first day of war, such hopes were dead."

While one can understand the reasons why the Americans had been taken by surprise at Pearl Harbor, their failure to take greater precautions to defend Clark Field is unfathomable. The defeat suffered there has been the subject of much controversy, and the officers responsible for decisions that morning offered conflicting accounts of what transpired. Word of the bombing of Pearl Harbor reached American officers in the Philippines about nine hours before the Clark Field raid, which occurred just after noon on December 8 (Philippine time). Expecting such an attack, the U.S. command had ordered the base's 35 bombers and 107 fighter planes into the air. Japanese bombing of other parts of the islands had already confirmed that they would not spare the Philippines. After remaining in the air for three hours, the bombers returned to Clark Field and were neatly lined up without any consideration of the possibility of an imminent attack—this despite the fact that a Japanese air force of some 500 aircraft was reported to be moving toward Manila.

For their part, the Japanese were apprehensive about the Clark Field raid. Their bombers had been delayed for several hours because of fog at their base in Taiwan, so they expected the U.S. command in the Philippines to be prepared. Instead, they found the U.S. Aircraft at Clark Field convenient targets. The result was the elimination of American air power from the western Pacific.

The attackers pressed their advantage by launching air strikes against other installations and landing troops at several points on the islands. The landings met with little effective resistance; the defense of the coast had been assigned to the 100,000-man Philippine reserve units, which were poorly trained and inadequately equipped. The regular American-Philippine army, which totaled about 31,000 men, was concentrated in the Manila area. Within two weeks, the Japanese controlled the air and sea and were established on Luzon as well as other islands. Faced with the realization that his dream of repelling the invaders at the shores had failed and that Manila was threatened, MacArthur fell back on the original war plans for defending the islands. On December 24, he ordered military personnel to withdraw to the Bataan Peninsula and established his headquarters at Corregidor. In the jungles of Bataan—the twenty-five-mile-long peninsula on the northern approach to Manila Bay—and on the small island fortress of Corregidor, the Americans and Filipinos prepared for a final defense.

The defenders held off the initial Japanese attacks on Bataan, but time was on the side of the attackers. About 100,000 American and Philippine military personnel and civilians now crowded into the peninsula, straining supplies of food and medicine. As it became evident that reinforcements would not be forthcoming, the morale of the defenders suffered. Likewise, they resented the fact that on March 12 MacArthur (under orders from President Franklin D. Roosevelt) and a large part of his staff were evacuated to Australia. As he departed, MacArthur dramatically promised, "I shall return"—notably not "We shall return." Unimpressed by such theatrics, troops on Bataan began to refer to him as "Dugout Doug." Desperate for food, the Americans and Filipinos slaughtered the horses and mules of the cavalry units; they also resorted to devouring monkeys, snakes, and water buffalo, as well as virtually all edible vegetation on the peninsula. Malnutrition and unsanitary conditions caused widespread outbreaks of disease, including malaria, beriberi, dysentery, and hookworm. The frustration of the troops was reflected in their adopted song:

> We're the battling Bastards of Bataan:
> No mama, no papa, no Uncle Sam;
> No aunts, no uncles, no cousins, no nieces;
> No pills, no planes, no artillery pieces.
> . . . And nobody gives a damn!

In the meantime the Japanese troops commanded by General Masaharu Homma received reinforcements. (Expecting another easy victory, the Japanese had initially committed a relatively small force to the Bataan campaign.) On April 3, 1942, they launched an offensive. The American and Philippine troops were too weak to mount a resistance, but standing orders from Washington and from MacArthur in Australia prohibited surrender. MacArthur cabled Lieutenant General Jonathan Wainright, who had become commander of forces in the Philippines following his evacuation: "I am utterly opposed under any circumstances or conditions to the ultimate capitulation of this command. If food fails you will prepare and execute an attack upon the enemy." Wainright relayed that order to Major General Edward P. King, who commanded the forces on Bataan. King soon faced the dilemma of whether to obey an order that would result in the slaughter of his forces or to surrender, which offered the only hope for the survival of his men. He chose to disobey orders, and on April 9 King surrendered.

King's army of some 80,000–100,000 starving and disease-ridden men, of whom about one-seventh were Americans and the remainder were Filipinos, was the largest U.S. Army ever to surrender. The Japanese commander assurred King that the prisoners of war would be treated well; he said, "we are not barbarians." In fact, the ensuing forced "march" of the POWs, what became known as the Bataan Death March, was among the most barbaric acts of the war. The Japanese forced their captives to walk sixty miles in intense heat and in deep dust to a POW camp. Deprived of almost any food or water, prisoners who failed to keep pace were shot, bayoneted, beheaded, or run over by trucks. The sides of the raod were littered with bodies. One survivor recalled:

"If you could not keep up with the group in the Death March, rather than slow the Death March, they'd get rid of you by shooting you. . . . Oh, they bayoneted people, they shot people. If they thought that you were delaying the Death March, you're dead." Another American remembered the day he was captured; "The first thing I did was to receive a good beating. As I was marched down that road, I passed my battalion commander . . . he had been tied to a tree and he was stripped to the waist and he was just covered with bayonet holes. He was dead obviously. And he had bled profusely. He had been bayoneted many, many times. And that's when I knew we were in for deep trouble." Another American recalled how some desperately thirsty POWS would break ranks to get to puddles of contaminated water along side the road that had been wallowed in by caribous; "the Americans and the Filipinos would actually lap up that water like a kitten would lap up milk. Many of them became very ill as a result. Several who broke ranks . . . would be shot by the Japanese. I saw a beheading of a Filipino who had broke ranks and ran for that type of water. So killings, yes, we saw a number of them along that march at different places."

About 54,000 prisoners sruvived this horrific experience and reached their destination. The death toll is difficult to estimate since several thousand POWs managed to escape into the jungle. The number of POWs who were shot, bayoneted, disemboweled, or beaten to death—or who died of malnutrition, starvation, or tropical disease—is generally placed at between 7,000 and 14,000, about one-third of whom were Americans.

Meanwhile, the remaining American and Filipino forces prepared to defend the island of Corregidor at the mouth of Manila Bay, which, ironically, was the scene of a great naval victory in 1898 that had led to U.S. control of the Philipines. Corregidor had extensive fortifications and an elaborate tunnel system that offered protection from aerial and artillery attack. But Corregidor could not survive the siege and bombardment that began with the fall of Bataan. As on Bataan, the Americans and Filipinos on Corregidor suffered from a shortage of food and water. At last the Japanese landed troops on the islands. Although the defenders fought valiantly, they could not withstand the advance.

As the Japanese approached the tunnels of Corregidor, where the remnants of the Philippine-American army held out, Wainright concluded that the time had come to surrender. The 11,000 men under his command faced certain death if the battle were to continue. On May 6 he surrendered the last of the American forces in the Philippines. In a message to Roosevelt and MacArthur, Wainright described his emotions as he prepared to meet the Japanese commander "with broken heart and head bowed in sadness but not in shame. . . ."

The defense of the Philippines has been criticized from various perspectives, which mostly focus on the decisions of General MacArthur. Critics have not contended the islands could have been held, but they have found that MacArthur's failure to assess the situation accurately led to decisions that weakened defense and hastened defeat.

First, MacArthur's prewar plan to defend the entire coast was based (in the words of his biographer D. Clayton James) on "unjustified optimism as to the abilities of himself, his staff, and the untried Filipino soldiers [which] unfortunately became a contagion . . . ultimately affecting even the War Department and the Joint Army and Navy Board." Although the United States in 1940–41 had increased its military support of the Philippines, the Philippine army lacked the capacity to defend the entire coast.

Second, in the confusing events surrounding the Japanese raid on Clark Field on the first day of the war, MacArthur, as commanding general, must be held responsible for leaving the air force vulnerable. His orders that morning were contradictory and indecisive. "When all the evidence is sifted, however contradictory and incomplete it may be," James has concluded, "MacArthur still emerges as the officer who was in overall command in the Philippines that fateful day, and he must therefore bear a large measure of the blame."

Third, MacArthur, despite overwhelming evidence to the contrary, seemed incapable of accepting the fact that the Philippines would not be reinforced. The priority, as prewar plans had determined, was given to the war in Europe: the devastating effects of the Pearl Harbor and Clark Field raids and the loss of Wake Island and Guam eliminated American air and naval power from the western Pacific. The Philippine defenders were left isolated in an area in which the Japanese held predominance. MacArthur's failure to accept the desperate nature of the situation delayed his decision to fall back on the original war plans to defend only Bataan and Corregidor, which, if ordered earlier, would have permitted a more orderly withdrawal and facilitated the supplying of food, medicine, and other necessities. "MacArthur managed to get his army back to Bataan," the historian C. P. Willmott has commented, "but did so at the cost of neglecting sound administrative arrangements that alone would have enabled it to function effectively on the peninsula. . . . The defenders of Bataan had to be placed on half-rations from the time they entered the peninsula. This situation had been avoidable, and the effects of delay were disastrous. . . . The Americans . . . had to turn to face . . . the three most successful generals in history. . . . Their names were Hunger, Disease, and Despair."

Finally and most fundamentally, MacArthur refused to believe that the Philippine Islands could be lost. Beyond his opposition to the surrender of Bataan, MacArthur also criticized Wainright's decision to surrender Corregidor. Earlier, when MacArthur left the islands, he went unwillingly and under the illusion that he would soon be put in command of a large army with which he could return in triumph.

How can his behavior be explained? MacArthur had a deep sense of responsibility to the Philippines, where he had served at several points during his distinguished career. An ambitious and arrogant man, MacArthur was unquestionably a brave soldier and had earned a reputation as a brilliant military strategist. He could not accept the loss of his adopted homeland, the Philippines. His energies were now devoted to one mission: the fulfillment of his promise to return, which, as biographer Carol Petillo writes, "became his obsession—and his redemption."

Despite the shortcomings of MacArthur's leadership, the defense of the Philippines had its positive effects. At a time when the other Western powers offered only token resistance to the Japanese, allowing relatively small Japanese armies to overrun Southeast Asia, the Americans and Filipinos fought bravely, giving a boost to Allied morale. The United States' decision to defend the islands for as long as it could reinforced Philippine-American solidarity. Certainly, many Filipinos resented the inadequacy of American reinforcements and some would later collaborate with the Japanese during the period of Japanese rule, but the common defense of Bataan and Corregidor sustained pro-American sentiment in the Philippines throughout the war. Among the many countries occupied by Japan, the most effective anti-Japanese guerrilla resistance campaign was that waged in the Philippines. The Filipinos' identification with the Allied cause drew from the common initial resistance against Japan and, more fundamentally, on the relatively liberal American rule and the promise of independence. Finally, the defense of the Philippines, even if short lived, forced the Japanese to commit additional troops to secure victory on Bataan and Corregidor, and delayed their control of Manila Bay—one of the most important harbors in the Pacific—for six months.

Popular Perceptions and Expectations

The rapid succession of Axis victories left the American public profoundly disappointed, but in no sense defeated. While many people in 1940–41 had expected the United States to be drawn into the war, they were not prepared for the momentous challenge that the nation faced by the spring of 1942. At first the Pearl Harbor attack had generated popular exhilaration, underscored by war rallies, bond drives, and the rush of men to join the armed services. There came the first of the war jingles, "We're going to have to slap—the sneaky little Jap." Roosevelt encouraged this buoyant mood. "He expressed the nation's optimism about victory," Roosevelt's biographer, James MacGregor Burns, has written, "but without the harsh warning of early defeats and blood and tears that Churchill had sounded."

But in the face of losses in the Atlantic, Mediterranean, North Africa, Russia and Asia, the early euphoria could not be sustained. The defeats sobered Americans; no one could escape the fact that this was going to be a long, difficult, and costly struggle.

Yet throughout the bleakest days of the war, Americans remained confident of victory. In public opinion polls taken from December

1941 to March 1942, the vast majority of Americans (85–90 percent) projected an Allied victory. Only 4 percent responded that the "Axis have a pretty good chance to win the war."

The defeats in the Pacific aroused deep emotions and astonished a people who prior to the Pearl Harbor attack had tended to discount Japan's military power. A public opinion poll in late November 1941 asked Americans which side would win a war between the United States and Japan; only 1 percent answered Japan, while 93 percent expected an American victory. More significant, most respondents expected that defeating Japan would be "comparatively easy" rather than "difficult." Japan's conquests shattered such illusions and it quickly became evident that it was going to take more than a "slap" to vanquish the Japanese. Just several months later, in early 1942, two-thirds of the public acknowledged that defeating Japan would be "difficult." The popular outrage over the Pearl Harbor attack and subsequent Japanese conquests, especially of the Philippines, led many Americans to believe that the United States should concentrate its resources on the war in the Pacific. In a public opinion poll of March 1942, 62 percent replied that the United States should put most of its effort into the fight against Japan; only 21 percent favored concentrating on Germany.

Week after week of discouraging news from the various fronts left Americans in need of heroes. The defenders of Wake Island, Bataan, and Corregidor were publicized across the nation, as their courageous stands against the Japanese were relayed in newspapers, on the radio, and in movie theater newsreels. Because the Philippine campaign provoked especially strong sentiments among Americans, General MacArthur emerged as *the* military hero of the Pacific war. MacArthur's sense of the dramatic, combined both with his staff's efforts to promote his favorable public image and the circumstances under which he operated, provided the material for a military legend. When he arrived in Australia, MacArthur's famed statement elevated the popular mood by explaining Roosevelt's orders as "for the purpose, as I understand it, of organizing the American offensive against Japan, a primary object of which is the relief of the Philippines. I came through and I shall return." The phrase "*I shall return*" became a popular rallying cry.

In the United States, MacArthur was extravagantly praised. Headlines in leading magazines and newspapers described him as "Destiny's Child," "Lion of Luzon," "Hero of the Pacific," "Incredible Warrior." Distinctions ranged from the nation's highest award—the Medal of Honor—to those of various private groups, including selection as Number One Father of the Year for 1942. This hero-worship was exploited; people eagerly bought lapel buttons with MacArthur's picture, as well as a home movie about his life, *America's First Soldier*. Hastily written biographies appeared, the first of which was entitled *General Douglas MacArthur, Fighter for Freedom*, and were enthusiastically received. Some political leaders and journalists began a MacArthur-for-President movement. MacArthur ranked among the "most admired" of Americans throughout the war. When high school students were asked in November 1942 which Americans they considered to be "great," MacArthur and Roosevelt were each named by nearly 60 percent of them; no more than 6 percent of the students named any other person.

MacArthur's emergence as a national hero was ironic considering his inadequate leadership in the Philippine campaign. At the time, however, the general's contradictory directions on December 8 and his reluctance to effect the Bataan-Corregidor defense plan were not known to the public.

However hastily they may have seized upon MacArthur as a hero, Americans were acutely aware of the immense challenge facing the nation. In concluding a four-page, detailed summary of the war in mid-1942, the news magazine *Time* reminded its readers of the following realities:

> At the end of six months of war, the U.S. has:
>   Not taken a single inch of enemy territory,
>   Not yet beaten the enemy in a major battle of land,
>   Not yet opened an offensive campaign.
> The war, in short, has still to be fought, as far as the U.S. is concerned. The campaigns to date have all been won by the enemy. More serious still, allies China and Russia are today in acute danger.

These are the solemn facts. It is also a fact that the U.S. has done an amazingly vast and rapid job of preparation for the battles still to be won. Until they are fought, the war can be neither lost nor won.

CHAPTER THREE

The War in Europe: The Turn of the Tide

In late 1942 the war began to favor the Allies. At the battle of Midway in June, the Americans finally halted the Japanese navy. Later that year they undertook their first offensives in the Pacific and European theaters. They invaded Japanese-held Guadalcanal, beginning a prolonged battle for control of that strategic island. Meanwhile, British and American forces undertook campaigns to force the Axis from North Africa. Finally, on the Eastern Front, the German and Russian armies fought the decisive battle of Stalingrad.

In waging war against Germany, the United States, Britain, and the Soviet Union were united only by their common enemy. They frequently debated over the means they should use to defeat Germany. The Americans frequently were caught between conflicting Soviet and British strategic priorities. Military leaders at the time, and historians ever since, have questioned whether the resources of the Allies were used with full effectiveness as they took the initiative against the Axis on land, sea, and in the air.

The Debate over Strategy

Before December 7, 1941, American military planners had decided that in the event of war against both Germany and Japan, the

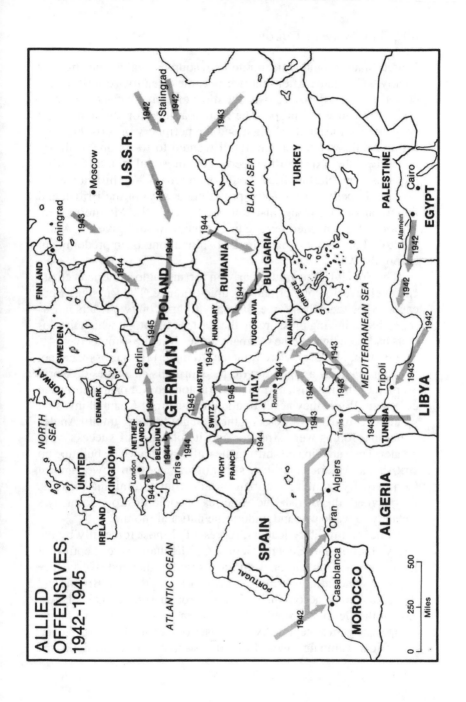

ALLIED
OFFENSIVES,
1942-1945

United States would concentrate its resources against the stronger enemy—Germany. After that war became a reality, Americans received conflicting advice over the most effective means to reverse Axis dominance in Europe. The British argued for "tightening the ring," which meant attacking along the periphery of Axis territory. Prime Minister Winston Churchill wanted to focus on North Africa, where the Axis position seemed the most vulnerable. Clearing the Axis from North Africa would open what Churchill called the "soft underbelly" of the Axis, providing a way for the British and Americans to move against Italy and secure the Mediterranean. A North African–Mediterranean campaign would give the Allies control of an area in which the British had long been predominant before the war.

The Soviet Union argued early on for an Anglo-American cross-Channel invasion of German-occupied France. The Russians were eager to see the Allies force Germany to fight on two fronts in Europe, thus relieving pressure on the Eastern Front, on which the Soviets had been fighting the Germans alone since the summer of 1941. The British, however, were reluctant to undertake a cross-Channel invasion. Fearing a repetition of the enormous casualties of World War I, they did not wish to rush into a prolonged war on the European continent. While they never doubted that a cross-Channel invasion would eventually be necessary, they sought to delay it until Anglo-American forces were stronger and its chances of success were greater. They anticipated shifting the military balance by building up British and American military strength and using air power against Germany. By bombing Germany's industrial and military centers, they argued, the British and Americans could destroy Germany's capacity to wage war and undermine national morale.

American military leaders, represented most forcefully by the Army chief of staff General George C. Marshall, were skeptical of British plans. Conventional military strategy dictated that victory required concentrating strength against strength. The British and Americans could accomplish this only through a cross-Channel invasion of the German stronghold in Western Europe, not by waging a campaign against the thin Axis defenses of North Africa. Moreover, an African campaign would divert resources from and delay the cross-Channel plan. With the outcome of Russian-German fighting in the east still in doubt, it seemed imperative for the British and Americans to take some risks to help the Russians withstand the latest German offensive. To skeptics, the British strategy amounted to pointless "pecking on the periphery" of the European war.

President Franklin D. Roosevelt, however, decided in favor of the North African campaign. The principal reason was political: he believed it essential that British and Americans seize the offensive against the Germans as early as possible. Marshall and other American military leaders believed that a cross-Channel operation would not be feasible until 1943. To Roosevelt, an offensive against the Germans within the first year of American involvement was essential to boost morale at home and to demonstrate strength and resolve. "The President," Marshall noted, "considered it very important to morale, to give the country a feeling they are in the war, to give the Germans the reverse effect, to have American troops somewhere in active fighting over the Atlantic." Beyond his interest in enhancing morale, Roosevelt was also persuaded to follow the North African strategy because of Britain's precarious position in the region. In the fighting on the Libyan desert in the summer of 1942, German and Italian forces overran the British at the battle of Tobruk, receiving the surrender of more than 28,000 British soldiers. The Axis powers, under the command of General Erwin Rommel, were now poised to advance toward the Suez Canal. To Roosevelt and some other U.S. strategists, the North African campaign offered a means of relieving pressure on the British in their effort to hold Egypt.

The North African Invasion

The Allied plan to gain control of northern Africa called for movements from both the east and the west. In the east, the British had to halt the Axis advance into Egypt and then push those forces back to Libya and ultimately force their surrender. This was a considerable challenge, given the strength of the Axis armies during their advance into Egypt in the spring of 1942.

In the west, Operation TORCH was to open a new front by the invasion and occupation of the French colonies of Morocco and

Algeria. This campaign involved combined American and British forces in a complicated and bizarre situation, resulting from the anomalous status of those colonies. Officials in Morocco and Algeria had proclaimed their neutrality in the war; hence, an Allied occupation meant that the British and Americans would be engaged in an unprovoked offensive against technically neutral states. The Allies, however, rightly considered those North African colonies as effectively serving the interests of Germany. Under the terms of the French-German armistice of June 1940, the collaborationist French government at Vichy had continued to administer France's African colonies. Colonial officials were thus loyal to Vichy and determined to avoid antagonizing Germany. So while Operation TORCH would be the first Allied offensive in the European theater, it would not entail landing in German-held territory. Rather the Allies would be trying to take control of countries administered by France, America's oldest ally. As the British and Americans planned for this operation, they were uncertain whether the French would resist or welcome the invaders.

The two-pronged action against the Axis in North Africa began with the renewal of Axis-British fighting in Egypt in late October 1942. For several months since Rommel's forces had penetrated deep into Egyptian territory, there was a pause in fighting while both sides reinforced their positions—the Germans preparing for a final thrust toward the Suez Canal, the British for a defense of their Egyptian foothold. The British were the more successful in securing reinforcements. Their navy and air force attacked the long Axis supply lines through the Mediterranean and North Africa, destroying about one-third of the supplies destined for Rommel's forces. Still, the Germans stood poised to take the Suez Canal, and Rommel's earlier successes against the British left much doubt about the ultimate outcome of the fighting in Egypt.

Then, on November 1 and 2, just a week after the renewal of the Axis-British fighting, the British broke through the German lines at the battle of El Alamein. Suddenly, Rommel's *Afrika Corps* was retreating into Libya, pursued by the British. For the first time since the war had begun three years earlier, the British enjoyed a major victory over the Germans. With their confidence restored, the British had at last turned the tide against the Axis in the fighting of the Egyptian and Libyan desert. Capturing the essence of this impressive victory, Churchill wrote: "The Battle of El Alamein was the turning point of British military fortunes. . . . Up to El Alamein we survived. After El Alamein we conquered."

Meanwhile, a large Anglo-American fleet gathered in the Atlantic and approached Morocco and Algeria. On November 8 some 90,000 troops (mostly American) scrambled ashore at several points along the North African coast. The invaders, commanded by General Dwight D. Eisenhower, encountered a confusing situation. From Vichy, Henri Pétain ordered his 120,000 French troops to resist. In some places the French fought the British and the Americans, while at others, they offered no resistance. After two days the Allies and Admiral Jean-François Darlan, commander of French forces, entered into an agreement whereby in return for ordering a cease-fire, Darlan would be recognized as having "responsibility for French interests in Africa."

Successful Anglo-American landings in Morocco and Algeria, combined with the British progress against Rommel beginning at El Alamein, signified that the British and the Americans had taken Axis-held territory for the first time in the war. Against that accomplishment one must balance three shortcomings of the campaign. First, the agreement with Darlan involved the Allies in a deal with a leading and especially notorious German collaborator. In England and in the United States, the "Darlan deal" was widely criticized. If the Allies were fighting a war against the evils of fascism, many persons asked, how could they have entered into an agreement with a man subservient to the Nazis? "Collaborating with a collaborator" stained the morality of the Allied cause.

In addition to this conflict between Allied ideals and practices, the "Darlan deal" infuriated the Free French movement, headed by General Charles de Gaulle, who had left France in 1940 to carry on the struggle against Germany from overseas. De Gaulle and his followers repudiated the collaborationist Vichy regime and regarded its leaders as traitors. The "Darlan deal" was defended by its supporters on the grounds of expediency; it ended the fighting and guaranteed French cooperation. The embarrassment of having Darlan as an associate of the Allies abruptly ended on Christmas Eve 1942, when a young Frenchman assassinated him. Later, responsibility for the administration of French territory in North Africa was transferred to a government in which de Gaulle was to become the dominant figure. Yet long after Darlan's death, the Allied deal with him continued to haunt the Allied relationship with the Free French.

Second, securing North Africa took much longer than the British and Americans had anticipated. After the Allied landings in Morocco and Algeria, Hitler rushed Axis forces to Tunisia, the other French colony in North Africa. (German forces also occupied the remainder of France at this time, thus eliminating the Vichy government.) When the British pursued the Germans from the east and the British-American force moved from Algeria and Morocco to attack Tunisia—the final Axis-held country in North Africa—they encountered strong resistance. It was not until the end of May 1943 that the Axis finally surrendered, at last bringing all of North Africa under Allied control. Not only did the North African operation require much time, but once the region was secured, the logical next step was to cross the Mediterranean and attack Sicily and Italy—the "soft underbelly." So in the summer of 1943, British and American units landed in Sicily. The Allies' relatively rapid victory on that island helped to undermine the support in Italy for Benito Mussolini, who fell from power on July 25. With Italy on the brink of surrender, the Allies now landed troops at Salerno on the Italian mainland, anticipating little resistance. By that time, however, Germany had rushed forces to Italy, so the Allies had to engage a strong enemy. Over the next year, the Italian campaign tied down thirty Allied divisions against twenty-two German divisions in mostly mountainous terrain. A significant consequence of the Italian campaign was the postponement of the cross-Channel invasion until the summer of 1944. In the meantime, Germany reinforced its defensive position along the coast of France.

Third, this delay in the cross-Channel invasion forced the Soviet Union to continue to bear the principal responsibility for fighting against the Germans. "What indeed," the historian Trumbull Higgins has asked, "had become of the concept of Germany first?" By following the strategy preferred by the British, the Anglo-American armies engaged only a limited number of German forces. In terms of the centers of German military strength in Europe, the North African–Mediterranean campaign was essentially peripheral. Higgins argued:

> Under the inspiration of this essentially British colonial type of war, it took an average of twelve divisions of the Western Allies some two and one-half years to push about the same number of Axis divisions back from northwest Egypt to northeast Italy, a distance of some two thousand miles over terrain chiefly distinguished by its poverty of good communications and its frequency of highly defensible positions. At the end of several bitterly contested campaigns the greatest natural barrier in Europe, the Alps, still lay between the Anglo-American armies and the Reich.

While the British and Americans pursued their Mediterranean campaigns, the Russians were facing about 180 German divisions. The Soviets, of course, had no choice but to fight against the armies that had invaded their country; the British and Americans had the option of deciding where and when to fight the Axis. Obviously, they chose an approach that failed to bring their full strength against the Germans. This decision not to force a Western Front was a source of increasing Russian bitterness toward its Western Allies. In its war against Germany between 1941 and 1945, the Soviet Union suffered enormous casualties: about 25 million were killed, two-thirds of whom were civilians. Understandably, the Soviets regarded a "real" second front — a cross-Channel invasion of France — as the true test of Anglo-American commitment to the defeat of Germany.

The Eastern Front: The Russian Victory at Stalingrad

As British and American forces engaged the Axis in North Africa, the long struggle on the Eastern Front between the German and Russian armies was reaching its decisive moment. At the battle of Stalingrad — waged from mid-November 1942 until the first days of February 1943 — the Soviets achieved a monumental victory that marked the turning point in the war against Germany.

Throughout the summer and fall of 1942, the prospects of Russian victory seemed remote as the Germans moved toward the objective—control of the oil-rich Caucasus area. Elsewhere on the long Russian-German front, the Germans engaged in a holding operation during 1942; victory in the south would make it possible to move later in the northern and central regions. As the Germans advanced, the city of Stalingrad—located on the Volga River and the industrial and communications center of the area—took on the utmost strategic significance. German control of the city would sever Soviet rail and water routes between the Caucasus and Moscow, weakening perhaps fatally Russian defenses in the north.

Hitler ordered part of his army in the south to capture Stalingrad. This fateful decision—"to chase two hares at once" (as Soviet Premier Josef Stalin described it)—divided a large force, leaving both halves vulnerable. The Soviets prepared to defend Stalingrad. Instructions from the German and Russian governments foretold the impending struggle. Hitler cautioned his generals that "the vital thing now was to concentrate every available man and capture as quickly as possible the whole of Stalingrad and the banks of the Volga." Meanwhile, the Russians were instructing the people of Stalingrad to "barricade every street, transform every district, every block, every house, into an impregnable fortress."

At first the two-pronged German offensive went according to plan, as its forces captured the first of the oil fields and entered the city of Stalingrad. But initial success was deceiving, for the Russian army and people were preparing for a fight to the death. Russian forces in the city, having been badly battered by the Germans throughout the 1942 campaign, received reinforcements, mostly coming across the Volga under cover of night. As Stalingrad held on, a large Soviet striking force amassed around the city; by mid-November, it outnumbered the Axis armies and enjoyed clear superiority in tanks and artillery. Considering the vulnerability of his army, which numbered about 250,000 men, the German commander, General Friedrich von Paulus, wanted to retreat to a more defensible winter line, but Hitler ordered Paulus to stand fast. The *Führer* would not tolerate any suggestion of weakness.

On November 19 the Russians attacked, trapping some 330,000 Axis troops. Paulus sought permission to break out of the encirclement, but again Hitler insisted that his armies complete the task of capturing Stalingrad. He shouted to his adviser, "I won't go back from the Volga!"

Following orders, the German army dug in, and for the next ten weeks the battle was waged in subfreezing temperatures and through severe snowstorms. The Germans had to receive supplies by air; they required 700 tons of food, equipment, ammunition, and medical supplies per day. Characteristically, General Hermann Goering, commander of the air force, promised Hitler that the Luftwaffe could provide the supplies. Yet from the beginning of the battle, the German air force lacked the capacity to relieve the ill-equipped, demoralized, and encircled army. For the first time in the year and a half of fighting on the Eastern Front, the Russians gained the military advantage. The bitter struggle went on throughout the winter. By January the Germans and Russians were fighting house to house, sometimes floor by floor, through the streets of Stalingrad; much of the combat was hand to hand. The historians Peter Calvocoressi and Guy Wint have described the inferno known as Stalingrad:

> By this time the city had turned into something which none of those who fought there had ever imagined and none who survived could ever forget. The closest and bloodiest battle of the war was fought among the stumps of buildings burnt or burning. From afar Stalingrad looked like a furnace, and yet inside it men froze. Dogs rushed into the Volga to drown rather than endure any longer the perils of the shore. The no less desperate men were reduced to automatons, obeying orders until it came their turn to die, human only in their suffering.

Having seen most of his once-proud army die as victims of combat, exposure, starvation, and suicide, Paulus finally defied Hitler's orders and ended the senseless struggle. On February 2 he surrendered the remaining 91,000 men of his army.

The Russian army celebrated a great victory. "The name of Stalingrad resounded all over the world," French historian Henri Michel has observed, "and Soviet historians rightly see the Red Army's brilliant success as the most crucial victory of the Second World War and one which marked its turning point." This "most crucial victory . . . and turning point" of the war against Germany was principally the result of a resurgence of Russian military power. Soviet industry had been reorganized and provided tanks, aircraft, artillery, arms, and other essentials for the Russian army. The struggle against the Germans stirred Russian patriotism, and the peoples of the Soviet Union united in what is known in Russia as the Great Patriotic War. This solidified the loyalty of the public to the government as had no event since the revolution of 1917 that had brought the communists to power. Strengthened by increased industrial productivity, a determined patriotism, and the swelled ranks of the army, the military leadership exploited the vulnerability of the German army, which lacked adequate support on its flanks as it advanced on Stalingrad. The Russians concentrated their forces in the region and launched the counteroffensive that trapped the Germans. The Soviets benefited from Hitler's pigheaded determination to take Stalingrad, which led him to dismiss all pleas from Paulus and military advisers to withdraw rather than suffer defeat, thus leaving the German army to its fate.

At most, the contribution of the British and Americans to the victory at Stalingrad was marginal. Western Allies in the North African campaign forced Hitler to transfer some of the Luftwaffe to the Mediterranean, and the possibility of a cross-Channel invasion meant that the Germans had to maintain large forces in Western Europe for the defense of that area. In addition, the British and Americans shipped some aircraft, tanks, and other supplies to the Soviets, but as yet, such support from Britain and the United States remained limited. Hence, the Russian pride in Stalingrad as a distinctive victory for their nation is, in no way, inappropriate.

Stalingrad was, in many ways, the "most crucial victory . . . and turning point." It demonstrated that the German army was not invincible, vastly improved Russian morale, and caused a serious loss of confidence among the German army and public. In Berlin, the German government proclaimed three days of national mourning over the fate of its army at Stalingrad. Meanwhile, the German army in the Caucasus began a retreat, pulling back some 375 miles within forty days.

The Germans made one major effort to recover. Hitler authorized an assault on the "Kursk bulge," an area on the long front about 450 miles northwest of Stalingrad where German forces surrounded the Soviets on three sides. Hitler's order underscored his determination to regain the initiative: "The victory of Kursk must have the effect of a lesson to the world." As Gerhard L. Weinberg writes in his history of the war, "He was quite right in this prediction, but not in the way he intended." In July 1943, the Germans attacked the Kursk bulge from the north and south, but the Soviets had anticipated the assault. Both sides depended heavily on armored units, and the fighting that continued for six days was the greatest tank battle in history. In the end, the Soviets achieved another major victory, confirming that the struggle on the Eastern Front had shifted decisively in their favor. That was the "lesson" of Kursk, the reverse of the one that Hitler had intended.

Elsewhere along the front the Russians took the initiative. By early 1943, they had begun to advance steadily against the Germans, forcing the invaders back to the west. Fighting on the Eastern Front remained as it had since June of 1941 — large armies incurring heavy losses of life on both sides while fighting over vast territories. The difference after Stalingrad, however, was profound: now, the Soviets were on the offensive.

The Battle of the Atlantic

Allied successes on land were reinforced by a dramatic change in the Battle of the Atlantic, but it was not until mid-1943 that the Allies gained naval ascendancy. Throughout 1942 and the first quarter of 1943, the Germans, principally through their U-boat force, continued to dominate naval warfare. They sank large numbers of Allied ships; in 1942 Allied losses totaled 7.8 million tons or 1,664 vessels, almost twice the volume of losses suffered the previous year. Admiral Karl Doenitz, the most outspoken advocate of submarine warfare, promised Hitler that with the completion of the buildup of the U-boat force, Germany would be capable of sinking 800,000 tons of shipping per month. Doenitz assured Hitler that the battle on the Atlantic was won. During each of three months in 1942 — March, June, and November — the Germans sank more than 800,000 tons of Allied shipping.

Incredibly, this did not bring a decisive victory. Just as the German naval strength reached its peak, Allied countermeasures gradually reversed the balance of the fighting on the Atlantic. To combat the attacks of the wolf packs (groups of German U-Boats), the Allies sent convoys comprised of supply ships surrounded by an escort of naval destroyers. Experience indicated that adequate protection required escorts to outnumber submarines by two-to-one. In 1942, however, a convoy of fifty merchant ships typically had only eight destroyer escorts to combat wolf packs of ten to fifteen submarines.

By late 1942, American shipyards working around the clock were constructing vessels faster than the U-boats could destroy them. Soon the convoy escort units were strengthened by the addition of aircraft carriers. This meant that by 1944 the typical fifty–merchant ship convoy was protected by as many as thirty escort ships. Long-range aircraft also were produced in sufficient numbers to patrol the Atlantic sea lanes. Allied advances in technology were also significant. The British and Americans devised a new airborne radar system that, unlike older longer-range radar, submarines could not foil with their radar detectors. This facilitated surprise air attacks when submarines surfaced. Sonar (sound navigation and ranging) systems, too, were improved, making it possible to detect submerged vessels. The Allies also developed more effective rocket-assisted depth charges and magnetic and acoustic antisubmarine torpedoes. No one of these changes would have been sufficient to shift the balance of naval warfare, but taken together they enabled the Allies to combat the U-boat fleet effectively for the first time.

Symptomatic of the changes on the Atlantic was German withdrawal from battles in which U-boat losses were high. Prior to the spring of 1943, the Germans had taken their toll on Allied shipping with minimal loss. But during May of 1943 alone, they lost forty-one U-boats—about one-third of the total at sea. The German high command abruptly halted submarine warfare, ordering the U-boats to return to their home ports. When the Germans renewed the submarine campaign, they suffered heavy losses. No longer were the notorious wolf packs a potent and virtually unstoppable threat. Altogether, 1,162 U-boats were commissioned during the war, 941 of which were sunk or surrendered.

Thus, by the middle of 1943 the Allies had gained an impressive and important victory on the Atlantic. This opened the way for greatly increasing the transport of supplies and of men, both of which were vital to the final defeat of Germany on the European continent. From this point forward, not a single ship transporting American troops to Europe was sunk.

Allied productivity and scientific ingenuity had achieved a triumph on the Atlantic, but in some ways, the Germans were responsible for their own defeat. Before the war, Hitler failed to build a large U-boat force. Had the German U-boat capability in 1939–40 been equivalent to the strength attained by early 1942, the results of the attacks on Allied shipping might well have been decisive and could have shut off the American supply lines to England and Russia completely. Instead, both sides raced throughout 1941 and 1942 to control the Atlantic. While the Germans enjoyed the ascendancy until early 1943, their earlier delay in building up their U-boat fleet gave the Allies time to outbuild and outnumber the German navy writ large, and to develop technologies and techniques that ultimately thwarted the submarine.

The Air War: The Bombing of Germany

At about the same time as they began to turn the tide in the Battle of the Atlantic, the British and Americans began mass bombings of Germany. By early 1943 the United States was able to use its air force effectively in Europe. Prior to that time, shortages of aircraft coupled with demands for air power in the Pacific and North African campaigns had prevented the Americans from joining fully with the British in the bombing of German targets. Operating from bases in England, the British and the Americans now undertook a large-scale bombing program.

The bombing operation was the subject of sharp differences between the British and Americans. The British saw air power as the key to victory. Churchill reflected the prevailing sentiment of British leaders when he stated in 1940: "The navy can lose us this war, but only the air force can win it." Large-scale bombing was seen as a way of avoiding the need to commit major armies to a ground war. By following the tactic of "area bombing"—indiscriminate raids against cities—the British expected not only to destroy German industrial capacity but, more important, the morale of the civilian population. This terror bombing was intended to level residential areas: one projection of such bombing said that by de-housing the population of Germany's largest cities, the Royal Air Force would "break the spirit of the people." Britain's experience during the "Battle of Britain," when the Luftwaffe attacked British cities, added a sense of revenge to the area-bombing campaign.

On the other side, the Americans preferred "precision bombing" directed against important industrial and military targets. Area bombing, in the opinion of American military leaders, wasted resources and produced uncertain results, and the Americans were skeptical that air raids undermined civilian morale. In the case of the British in 1940–41, the German air attacks had stiffened, not weakened, public morale. The Americans saw strategic bombing as an essential means of supporting ground operations rather than a means of winning the war by itself. Several months elapsed, however, before the Americans' precision bombing began to work effectively. During the early stages of the campaign, German fighters shot down many American bombers. For several weeks in late 1943 and early 1944, the American bombing was delayed until a newly developed long-range fighter, the P-51, was deployed and provided protection for the bombers.

What, then, were the results of the Allies' mass bombing campaign? With the British attacking by night and the Americans by day, the Allies destroyed Germany's industrial centers. One by one German cities were reduced to rubble. Allied bombers dropped 207,000 tons of bombs on greater Germany in 1943 and 915,000 tons in 1944. (By contrast, in 1942, the British had dropped 48,000 tons on Germany.) As the Americans predicted, area bombing did not destroy the morale of the German people. Like the British in 1940–41, the Germans withstood the terror of attack from the air. Nazi propaganda effectively exploited popular indignation over the indiscriminate bombing to exhort Germans to greater sacrifice for the homeland. Many military historians conclude that the bombing campaign would have accomplished more if the British had not placed such stubborn faith in the vulnerability of German morale.

The British campaign diverted resources from other needs and was a slow way to defeat Germany. Moreover, the bombings only marginally affected German industrial capacity, at least until the late stages of the war. German armament production continued to rise in 1943 and 1944, and it started to decline only during the last few months of the war. And, as the Americans had asserted, precision bombing proved more effective than area bombing. Albert Speer, German minister of armaments and munitions, later declared: "The American attacks which followed a definite system of assault on industrial targets, were by far the most dangerous . . . [and] caused the breakdown of the German armaments industry."

Yet it is also evident that mass bombing worked to the Allies' advantage in important ways. It forced the Germans to commit great numbers of their reduced manpower to the unending task of clearing bombed areas and reconstructing factories. By 1944 perhaps as many as 1.5 million people, including many skilled workers who were needed elsewhere, were assigned to reconstruction. Also, the mass bombing forced the German air force into a defensive position. The Germans had no choice but to build more fighters, which reduced significantly their ability to engage in bombing raids in support of their armies at the Eastern Front. By the time the British and Americans were actively planning their cross-Channel invasion of France in early 1944, German air power in that area was negligible. In sum, the bombing program forced the Luftwaffe to concentrate on protecting the homeland. And with the British and Americans outproducing the Germans in numbers of aircraft, the Germans were increasingly ineffective even in that task. The Allies had won the battle in the air.

The Cross-Channel Invasion: D-Day

The cross-Channel invasion of France on June 6, 1944 (code named D-Day), was, in the words of Winston Churchill, "the most difficult and complex operation that has ever taken place." The victories of the British and Americans in North Africa and the Mediterranean, on the Atlantic, and in the air, led inevitably to the major Anglo-American operation of the war: the cross-Channel invasion of

Hitler's "Fortress Europe." A large Allied army had been assembled in England. Now, somehow, those forces had to cross the English Channel, disembark in a heavily fortified area, and gain a foothold on the coast of France.

The invasion—Operation OVERLORD—was inherently hazardous. The Germans had constructed the Atlantic Wall, a line of fortifications, obstacles, and mines that stretched 2,500 miles along the western coast of France and the Low Countries. Fifty-eight German divisions, including ten *panzer* (tank) divisions that could swiftly deliver an armored counteroffensive, defended Western Europe. The Germans knew that the Allies would attempt an invasion; if it succeeded, Germany's fate was certain. In barracks and restaurants, the refrain of a popular song, "The Watch on the Channel," echoed:

> We stand in the West; we are fully prepared;
> Let the enemy come today.
> We are on guard, our fists are hard,
> We shall stand in the West at bay. . . .

How, exactly, to "stand in the West" divided the German command. Rommel, whom Hitler had brought to Europe to help hold the Atlantic Wall, argued that the Germans had to resist the invaders and prevent any successful landings; he had learned from his experiences in the Mediterranean that once the Allies established a foothold, it would be virtually impossible to dislodge them. On the other hand, Field Marshal Gerd von Rundstedt, commander of German troops in France, believed that the Germans should wait to ascertain exactly where the major invasion was taking place and then unleash their armored divisions against that point to repulse the Allied force back into the sea. This action would so demoralize the Allies, von Rundstedt maintained, that it might even reverse German fortunes elsewhere and bring victory. Hitler ultimately opted for a compromise strategy, which meant that the Germans spread their defenses along the west coast of France and failed to bring their full power against the initial invasion.

Beyond that questionable strategic decision, the German defense had other weaknesses. The lines of authority within the high command were not clear, and their naval and air support was no match for that of the Allies. Finally, the German ground forces, widely dispersed along the coast, were not at full strength and included weaker units that the Germans had hastily pressed into service.

The Allied Expeditionary Force (AEF), comprised of the landing force and its supply units, was under the command of General Eisenhower. During the North African campaign, Eisenhower had efficiently coordinated Allied strategy. In planning OVERLORD, with its much larger AEF, Eisenhower worked effectively with British and American commanders, including several egotistical "stars." British generals Bernard L. Montgomery and Alan Brooke were haughty, contemptuous of Americans generally, and condescending toward Eisenhower in particular. Among the American generals, the volatile, impulsive, and dogmatic George Patton resented Eisenhower's position. Montgomery, Brooke, and Patton, however, each had great military skill, and Eisenhower exploited each man's strengths while soothing each man's ego. No one questioned that Eisenhower was in charge. The result was an effective Anglo-American command team. The Eisenhower personality—symbolized by a broad grin and relaxed manner—projected self-confidence and optimism. In the summer of 1944, he faced his greatest command challenge.

OVERLORD required thorough and ingenious planning. From air reconnaissance and the French "underground," the Allies learned minute details of the terrain of northern France. Prior to D-Day, extensive bombing raids destroyed much of the German line of supply to its forces along the coast. All German airfields within a 125-mile radius of the coast were systematically bombed. After deciding that the invasion would take place along the Normandy coast, the Allied command deemed it essential to prevent the Germans from bringing their full strength to that area. Hence, the Allies undertook diversionary tactics to keep the Germans uncertain whether Normandy was the major invasion point. The absence of port facilities in Normandy necessitated the construction of prefabricated ports that had to be carried across the Channel and erected on the coast after it had been secured. The most unpredictable factor facing the Allies was the weather; an unexpected storm in the English Channel could have ruined the entire operation.

Indeed, bad weather forced postponement of plans to invade on June 5, but when weather reports indicated favorable conditions for the next day, Eisenhower gave the simple command—"Okay, we'll go"—to launch the largest amphibious invasion in history. Outwardly confident, Eisenhower privately feared failure. He prepared a statement to be released in the event of defeat: "Our landings . . . have failed to gain a satisfactory foothold and I have withdrawn the troops. . . . If any blame or fault attaches to the attempt, it is mine alone."

The Allies faced many risks as OVERLORD unfolded during the night of June 5 and early morning of June 6. A coded message sent by British radio instructed the French resistance to sabotage rail lines and roads throughout western France. Allied bombardment of the landing area began at midnight. During the early morning hours the first invaders—23,000 airborne troops—parachuted behind enemy lines.

Then, at the dawn of a gray and windy day, the large amphibious force landed 70,000 men on five beaches along the Normandy coast. Wading through waist-deep water, the Allied soldiers began the penetration of Hitler's Fortress Europe. Many men never made it ashore in the face of the dug-in German defenders. Yet within a few hours, the Allies, thanks to their overwhelming numbers and firepower plus support from air and sea, managed to secure footholds on the landing sites, with the British and Canadian forces put ashore at beaches code-named Gold, Juno, and Sword and the Americans at Utah and Omaha.

The landings at Omaha, however, were nearly disastrous. There, Allied operations were poorly coordinated and had inadequate support. From high cliffs the Germans pinned down the invading forces along the sea wall; the bodies of many victims thrashed about in the tempestuous waters of the Channel. On the beaches soldiers huddled in the midst of the bodies of their comrades. One commander radioed the situation succinctly, "They're firing down our throats." Somehow, the Americans had to clear the Germans from the bluffs. "Two kinds of people are staying on the beach," one colonel screamed to his men, "the dead and those who are going to die. Now let's get the hell out of here!" Paying for every foot gained with heavy casualties, the invaders painstakingly inched their way up the beaches and cliffs. By the end of a harrowing day, they had tenuously secured Omaha Beach.

As word reached the United States that the D-Day invasion had begun, people stopped their normal pursuits and most daily routines came to a standstill. Americans waited anxiously by their radios for reports from Europe. The news generated enthusiasm and relief. Fortress Europe had been breached and some 130,000 Allied troops had landed in Normandy.

Despite all of the Allied planning and their air and naval superiority, the invasion could easily have failed. Rommel had been right: the Allies had to be stopped on the beaches or not at all. Had his strategy been followed and had he been given more time to upgrade coastal defenses, the entire operation might have resembled the bloody epic at Omaha. On the day of the invasion, Germany's most renowned general was not even in France: Rommel had gone to Germany for consultations with Hitler. Moreover, had Hitler recognized that Normandy was the principal invasion point, the Germans could have rushed their panzer divisions to the area. There was irony in Hitler's reaction to the invasion: while earlier he (and Rommel) had guessed that Normandy would be the site of the major Allied invasion, once it began, Hitler became convinced that it was diversionary and that a second and larger invasion would take place farther east. Enemy miscalculations thus contributed to the Allied success.

The Normandy beachhead became the center of a massive buildup during the next seven weeks. By the end of July, nearly 1.5 million troops had been transported across the English Channel. The dimensions of this undertaking were staggering: the navy was transporting supplies at the rate of 6,000 tons per day. In late July the Allies broke out of the coastal perimeter. They began to push the Germans to the east. By the end of August, they had liberated Paris.

With the Russians pushing steadily toward Germany from the east and with the other Allies pressing from the west, many observers expected that the war would soon be over. Hitler, however, was planning a desperate gamble: a surprise attack in the hilly, densely wooded Ardennes region of Belgium and Luxembourg, which was lightly held by British and American forces. Throughout the fall of 1944, as the Allies paused and prepared for a spring campaign against the German homeland, the Germans secretly amassed 250,000 men and a large tank corps. Hitler saw an opportunity to reverse Germany's fortunes: a successful attack could give it control of badly needed fuels that were stored in Belgium and could be so demoralizing and devastating to the Western allies that Germany could concentrate on the Russians, who were fast approaching from the east. On December 16, the assault came and caught the Allies completely by surprise. The offensive was aided by fog and snowy weather, which kept Allied air forces grounded for nearly a week. The Germans advanced steadily, creating a triangular "bulge" sixty miles deep and fifty miles wide in the Allied lines. Eisenhower rushed reinforcements, totaling some 240,000 men, to the region. With a break in the weather, Allied planes inflicted heavy damage on German trains and armor. In frigid conditions on the ground, the Allied counteroffensive gained the upper hand and steadily reduced the "bulge," forcing the Germans into an increasingly narrowing sector. Accepting the folly of his gamble, Hitler on January 13, 1945, ordered a retreat.

The Battle of the Bulge cost Germany more than 100,000 men, 1,600 planes, 700 tanks—losses that undermined any prospect of halting the Allied attack on the homeland itself. The battle was also the bloodiest Americans experienced in the entire war. American forces suffered 89,500 casualties including 19,000 killed, 47,500 wounded, and 23,000 captured or missing. The 19,000 American dead were unsurpassed by those of any other engagement.

The Battle of the Bulge brought Hitler's Third Reich to the verge of collapse. Since the dark days of 1942, it had taken the Allies more than two years of fighting to approach the threshold of victory. To the peoples of Europe who had suffered so much since the war began in 1939, the New Year 1945 promised an end to the long struggle.

CHAPTER FOUR

The Pacific Theater: The War against Japan, 1942–1945

World War II as it was waged in Europe and Asia was, in many respects, two distinct conflicts. The ideological relationship was clear: the Allied powers were determined to defeat fascism as represented by the Axis Alliance. Clearly, military developments in one theater affected the other. But, on both sides, belligerents acted independently. The Germans and Japanese never coordinated strategy because their national interests dictated otherwise. Germany would have benefited from a Japanese attack on Russia or from a Japanese offensive across India and the Middle East, but Japan's leaders wanted to avoid war with the Soviet Union and believed their national survival necessitated concentrating resources in the Pacific and Southeast Asia.

Among the Allies, only the United States played a major role in both Europe and Asia. Given their preoccupation with the struggle against Germany, Britain contributed little to the war against Japan, and the Soviet Union did not declare war on Japan until August 8, 1945—shortly before the Japanese surrendered. The United States thus assumed responsibility for the Allied war effort in Asia. Unlike the war in Europe, where American operations were continually questioned by other principal Allied powers, in the Pacific the

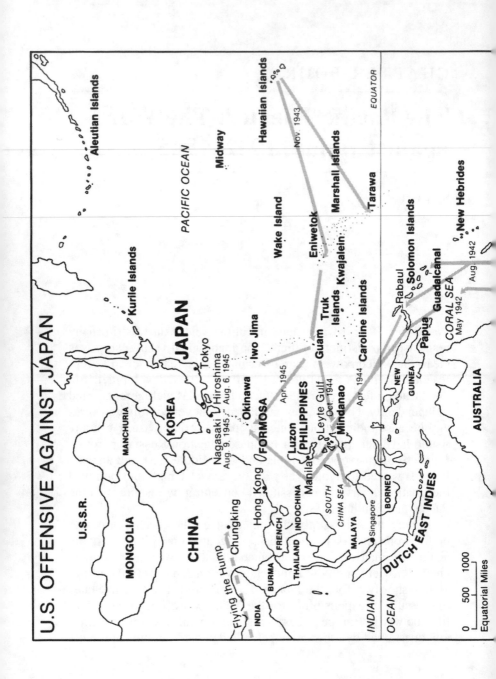

U.S. OFFENSIVE AGAINST JAPAN

U.S.S.R.

MONGOLIA

MANCHURIA

CHINA

KOREA

JAPAN

Tokyo

Hiroshima Aug. 6, 1945

Nagasaki Aug. 9, 1945

Flying the Hump

Chungking

Hong Kong

BURMA

THAILAND

FRENCH INDOCHINA

MALAYA

Singapore

SOUTH CHINA SEA

BORNEO

Kurile Islands

FORMOSA

Okinawa

Luzon

Manila

PHILIPPINES

Leyte Gulf Oct. 1944

Mindanao

Apr. 1945

INDIA

INDIAN OCEAN

0   500   1000

Equatorial Miles

DUTCH EAST INDIES

NEW GUINEA

AUSTRALIA

Apr. 1944

Aleutian Islands

PACIFIC OCEAN

Midway

Hawaiian Islands

Nov. 1943

EQUATOR

Wake Island

Marshall Islands

Tarawa

Eniwetok

Kwajalein

Guam

Truk Islands

Caroline Islands

Iwo Jima

Rabaul

Solomon Islands

New Hebrides

Aug. 1942

Guadalcanal

Papua

CORAL SEA

May 1942

United States fought on its own terms. While Britain, Australia, and others were also at war with Japan, only the United States could challenge Japan's dream of political and economic predominance over East Asia and the Pacific. It was American military strength that determined the war against Japan.

"Our War": Characteristics and Popular Perceptions

In view of the clear Japanese-American focus of the Asian war and the emotional reaction to the Pearl Harbor attack, the American public identified very closely with the war against Japan. In sum, Americans saw the Pacific theater as "our war."

The war in the Pacific was fought differently from the one in Europe in that it was primarily a naval conflict, with a limited role of the army on both sides. The Japanese had built their empire through effective use of naval power. The success of the Japanese fleet in the Pearl Harbor attack established the basis of the war. It was naval strength that brought Japan to its position of predominance in Asia and the Pacific. To preserve the empire, Japan relied on naval supremacy, which it enhanced by fortifying a number of small, strategically located islands.

To challenge the Japanese, the Americans had to build up their navy, especially aircraft carriers from which to dispatch bombers to attack Japanese-held islands. Much of the fighting—certainly the most decisive—was for control of islands in the Pacific. This meant that unlike the war in Europe, where fighting on land was all but continuous, the fighting in the Pacific was sporadic. What land battles took place were especially bitter and bloody, and usually waged in the intense heat of jungles. With the end of one island battle, however, a break in land fighting followed while preparations were made for the next invasion.

War in the Pacific had strong racial overtones, which contributed to the barbarity with which it was fought. The Japanese victories of 1941–42 came at the expense and humiliation of the Western imperial powers—Britain, France, the Netherlands, and the United States. Never before had an Asian nation so overwhelmed the white race, thus shattering the myth of the West's military superiority that had buttressed its political hold on Asia. Many Asian peoples, even some who deeply distrusted Japan's intentions, took a measure of pride in Japanese military accomplishments. In many of the areas that Japan conquered, it found native leaders, who earlier had worked on behalf of the Western powers, willing to collaborate with the New Order. In all of the former Western colonies, the Japanese stimulated nationalism and a determination to prevent the white man's return. The Japanese themselves proved to be just as exploitive and insensitive as the white imperialists they replaced, but the resultant anti-Japanese feeling did not mean that the peoples of Southeast Asia were prepared to welcome the return of Western imperialists. The damage to Western dominance had already been done; by the end of the war, the peoples within the Japanese Empire only wanted to be free from any kind of foreign domination.

"Our war" meant that Americans carried a more intense outrage into fighting against Japan than against the Germans. Nearly one-half of the fighting men responded positively to the statement "I would really like to kill a Japanese soldier." In contrast, less than 10 percent of combatants reacted the same way to the statement, "I would really like to kill a German soldier." A hatred of the Japanese had derived from the Pearl Harbor attack and the Bataan Death March, making the Japanese the "number one enemy." In a sample of American public opinion taken in early 1942, two-thirds of respondents favored concentrating military efforts against Japan; only 25 percent favored giving priority to the European war. The Japanese were seen as the most barbaric and inhumane of peoples. For instance, when Americans were asked in another 1942 public opinion poll to select from a list of twenty-five adjectives the words that most applied to the Japanese, the predominant responses (those identified by more that 50 percent) were "treacherous, sly, [and] cruel." During the war Americans always referred to the enemy by the racially derogatory word, "Japs." The tendency to attribute Japan's aggression to national characteristics is striking when compared with popular attitudes toward German character and behavior. Polls taken in June 1943 asked with which of the following statements interviewees most agreed were expressions of Japanese and German national character:

	Percent agreeing on Japan	Percent agreeing on Germany
1. "They will always want to go to war to make themselves powerful."	57%	27%
2. "They may not like war, but have shown that they are too easily led into war by powerful leaders."	25%	34%
3. "They do not like war and if given the same chance as other people, they would become good citizens of the world."	11%	38%
4. Don't know.	7%	3%

The Japanese were subject to racial stereotyping. In cartoons and various forms of propaganda, they were commonly depicted as yellow-faced, toothy rats. Comic strip heroes took on the Japanese as their wartime enemies; the Japanese were seen as subhuman—all teeth and spectacles—and no match for Americans. In a parade to raise war bond contributions, one float appeared bearing the heading, "Tokyo—We are Coming"; on it, a large American Eagle was leading a torrent of bombs against a herd of yellow rats who were desperately trying to escape.

In newspapers, magazines, books, and on the radio, the war in the Pacific was seen as a struggle between barbaric Japanese and gallant Americans. Typical was *Men on Bataan* by John Hersey, which helped create the image of General Douglas MacArthur as a military genius and portrayed his beleaguered followers in heroic terms. In this and countless other stories, Americans came to see the GI as a reluctant warrior—an average, clean-living young man from a small town whose patriotism led him to fight a war in tropical jungles against a bestial enemy.

Films about the war (a disproportionate number of which dealt with battles in the Pacific) continually reinforced popular images and racial hatred. From the early days of the nation's participation in the war, Americans managed to find inspiration in the heroic defenses of Wake Island and the Philippines. Films depicting those battles glorified Americans even in defeat by reminding audiences of previous military victories and the reasons why the United States was fighting the Axis. An American surrender was never shown, so that such films typically ended as a badly outnumbered band of Americans fired their last rounds of gunfire at the approaching Japanese. The first such film, *Wake Island*, dramatized the defense of that outpost and appealed widely to audiences throughout the country. The cinematic American defenders of *Wake Island* uttered such memorable phrases as, "There are no atheists in foxholes," and, in a reminder of earlier defenders of freedom, "Don't shoot until you see the whites of their eyes."

There followed quickly a number of films depicting the loss of the Philippines, always in ways that made the outcome seem tolerable and meaningful. By making a determined last stand against the Japanese, the Americans were seen as having achieved a tactical victory by tying up thousands of enemy troops, thus delaying their advance elsewhere and winning valuable time for the Allies. That idealism did not fit with the facts: Japan's advance in 1942 was not significantly affected by American resistance in the Philippines. The Filipinos, who constituted most of the actual forces resisting the Japanese, were often not evident and Americans were never seen as surrendering (when, in fact, many did surrender). Instead, they were shown fighting to the last man. At the end of one Philippines-based film, the American commander shouts to the enemy as his outnumbered forces prepare for their last stand: "Come on suckers! What are you waiting for? We'll be here. We'll always be here. Why don't you come and get us?" In closing, he says quietly, "It doesn't matter where a man dies, so long as he dies for freedom."

Whether the setting was the Philippines or one of the remote islands, the Japanese were always seen by American moviegoers as senseless, brutal killers. In one scene in which Japanese planes are attacking a hospital, an American exclaims: "They're machine gunning! They're strafing! The beasts! The slimy beasts!" And wherever the battle, the Japanese were opposed by an American fighting unit that reflected a cross section of the United States population. The

American unit typically included one small-town Anglo-Saxon, a Jew, a southerner, and a mixture of second-generation Irish, Poles, and Italians (one invariably from Brooklyn).

Reinforcing the anti-Japanese sentiment was a wholly sympathetic view of China and its people. This pro-Chinese feeling had originated long before Pearl Harbor and can be traced to an American sense of attachment to the Chinese, resulting from large-scale missionary activity in China during the late nineteenth and early twentieth centuries. Most important, from the time of Japan's attack on China in 1937, Americans sympathized with the Chinese cause; public opinion polls between 1937 and 1941 indicated overwhelming popular support for the Chinese. After Pearl Harbor, American identity with the Chinese cause became even stronger, for the Chinese were now seen as a valued ally. The press and other media fostered the impression that the Chinese under the leadership of General Chiang Kai-shek and his American-educated wife were fighting valiantly against the Japanese. Chiang was commonly depicted as building a strong and democratic China, which would collaborate with the United States in winning the war and preserving peace in Asia afterward. (Americans may have admired the Chinese, but they had only a sketchy idea of where China was located. In a 1942 poll, 60 percent of the public could not find it on a map of the world.)

Midway: The End of Japan's Naval Invincibility

In the first week of June 1942—six months after Pearl Harbor— the Japanese and American navies clashed at the Battle of Midway Island, where Japan pressed its military advantage and the United States sought to reestablish its naval strength. Like many battles, the outcome at Midway reflected the quality of planning on both sides.

Having established control over Southeast Asia, China, and the western Pacific, Japan's leaders had to address the question: Where to advance next? Some officials favored further expansion into the Indian Ocean, which might lead to the conquest of the Middle East and the linking of the Japanese with the German army (which was then advancing across North Africa toward the Suez Canal). Other

Japanese officials wanted to renew attacks in the South Pacific in order to invade Australia or at least completely isolate that nation from the other Allies. While those alternatives each had attractive features, the most compelling case was made for resuming the naval thrust across the central Pacific, thus crippling America's capacity to challenge Japan's New Order. The chief advocate of this approach was Admiral Isoroko Yamamoto, who enjoyed immense prestige as the architect of the Pearl Harbor victory. Accordingly, the decision was made to undertake an invasion of Midway.

Midway—a coral island six miles in diameter and only partially composed of dry land—was strategically important. The United States recognized this long before the famous battle; the Navy had occupied Midway in 1867 and established a base there. Located about 1,100 miles northwest of Pearl Harbor, Midway was the key to control of the Hawaiian Islands.

For the Midway offensive, Yamamoto mustered a large fleet, altogether some 200 vessels, including 11 battleships, 8 carriers with a strength of 700 aircraft, 22 cruisers, 65 destroyers, and 21 submarines. The move against Midway had two objectives: to occupy the island from which the Japanese could threaten the Hawaiian Islands and even the Pacific coast of the United States; and to draw the remnants of the American fleet into a battle that would finish the destruction begun at Pearl Harbor. Moreover, the capture of Midway promised to enhance Japan's security. In April 1942 a surprise American bombing raid against Tokyo, led by Lieutenant Colonel James H. Doolittle, had been launched from carriers in the Pacific; the incident alarmed Japan's leaders and reminded them of their vulnerability to air attack. To help ensure success of the mission at hand, Yamamoto sent part of Japan's fleet in the direction of the Aleutian Islands off the coast of Alaska; this was a diversionary tactic employed to draw part of the American fleet away from Midway. In view of their series of easy victories and their naval superiority, Japan's leaders were confident of another victory as its fleet, with Yamamoto in command, prepared to attack Midway.

On the American side, the navy under Admiral Chester W. Nimitz was aware of Japan's plans. American cryptanalysts had broken the Japanese code; this deciphering of messages meant that the Americans were aware that the main Japanese objective was Midway and that the Aleutian force was only a decoy. The navy thus concentrated on the defense of Midway, but the United States had far fewer vessels at its disposal than those in the attacking force. A U.S. force of three carriers, eight cruisers, and fifteen destroyers was assembled to confront the Japanese. (Recognizing the urgency of the situation, the navy pressed workers in the shipyards at Honolulu to get the badly damaged carrier *Yorktown* into combat-ready condition quickly; despite estimates that repairs would take two months, the *Yorktown* was actually repaired in three days and sent into battle.)

Assuming that the attack would catch the Americans by surprise, Yamamoto ordered the air attack that began on June 4. For a few hours, Japanese calculations appeared to be correct. The American installations on Midway were destroyed, and the island probably could have been taken if the Japanese had launched an invasion immediately. Yet the key factor was that the United States was prepared to meet the offensive head-on. American aircraft intercepted Japanese planes as they returned from Midway (downing forty-three planes before they could reach safety) and also attacked the Japanese carriers. In the course of a very long day of fighting, the Japanese never recovered. Combat in the skies west of Midway resulted in the sinking of four Japanese carriers, without which Japan's overall numerical superiority counted for little. Now Yamamoto ordered a retreat.

The Japanese attack on Midway had failed. Japan had accomplished neither of its objectives. The island remained in American hands, and the American fleet had suffered only minimal losses. The comparative losses tell the story:

	U.S.	*Japan*
Casualties	307	2,500
Carriers	1	4
Cruisers	0	1
Destroyers	1	0
Aircraft	147	332

A major reason for this outcome was that Nimitz, aware of Japan's plans, was able to concentrate his naval power—limited as it was—to meet the attack.

Also contributing to the outcome of the Battle of Midway were mistakes committed by the Japanese before launching the attack. Their leaders had failed to adhere to some basic considerations of military planning, as they had two conflicting objectives: their strategy for capturing a target was hardly the most effective way of destroying the American fleet. Had the Japanese concentrated on the latter objective, Midway would likely have fallen without much of a fight. Erring again, the Japanese failed to exploit their naval superiority. Had Yamamoto massed his forces against the primary target rather than dispersing them, the day might have been his. The diversionary move toward the Aleutians not only failed to draw the American fleet away from Midway, but it also deprived Yamamoto of ships badly needed at Midway.

Compounding their errors, the Japanese had underestimated their enemy. They assumed that surprise could be achieved as easily as it had been at Pearl Harbor. But this thinking ignored the impact of the Pearl Harbor attack on American commanders in the Pacific; having been fooled once, they were now doubly alert. Finally, the Japanese failed to make contingency plans since they never anticipated any difficulties. Unprepared, they lost their nerve when their carriers were unexpectedly hit by the Americans, and so they were forced to abandon the engagement.

In view of the precision and thoroughness of Japan's earlier naval warfare, how can one explain these failures at Midway? The answer may simply be that the Japanese suffered from overconfidence. Their naval victories in the Pacific had to that point been painless, and those successes led to a certain carelessness in planning and execution at Midway. Yamamoto and other commanders deluded themselves into thinking that the prize of Midway would be plucked readily from an outnumbered, shocked, and dispirited American fleet. The victories beginning on December 7 had thus created arrogance and blind optimism.

The loss at Midway shattered the illusion of Japan's naval invincibility. Thomas W. Zeiler writes in his history of the war that "Midway made the central Pacific safe from further Japanese offensives; the Imperial Navy lost the initiative and never regained it."

Guadalcanal: The First Offensive

Following its defeat at Midway, Japan revised its plans. Now, instead of challenging the United States in the central Pacific, Japan's forces would refocus on the southwest Pacific by encircling Australia. This was to be accomplished through two routes: the capture of all of New Guinea and the establishment of a base at its southeastern tip, Port Moresby; and the seizure of the Solomon Islands focusing on Guadalcanal—an island of 2,500 square miles at the southeastern tip of that island chain—where they planned to construct an air base. With those two bases operational, the Japanese could move against Australia.

American commanders recognized the importance of this new Japanese movement, for the enemy's control of Guadalcanal would have cut the Allied supply lines to Australia. In Washington, Admiral Ernest J. King, chief of naval operations, urged a countermove against Japan. Some British and American officers opposed the plan, maintaining that it undermined the basic "Europe-first" strategy; the United States, they believed, should fight only a holding operation in the Pacific. Overruling such reservations, the Joint Chiefs of Staff on July 2, 1942, authorized Operation WATCHTOWER—the capture of the Solomon Islands. Within a few days the operation became a reality, for American reconnaissance planes reported that the Japanese were indeed constructing an airfield on Guadalcanal. Time was of the essence if the Japanese were to be prevented from having a fully operational air base, and the determined King—described by his daughter as "the most even-tempered man in he navy—he is always in a rage"—ordered that WATCHTOWER begin within the month.

Guadalcanal typified the small, tropical islands on which Americans and Japanese were to fight many battles. The climate was constantly hot and humid on the malaria-ridden island. The sandy beaches dotted with coconut palms abruptly gave way to mountainous, dark-green, rain forest. From the ground came the stench of decaying vegetation.

The Japanese and American roles at Guadalcanal were the reverse of those at Midway, for this time the United States was on the offensive. As it planned its first amphibious invasion since the Spanish-American War forty-four years earlier, the American naval command hardly had reason for optimism. Among officers in the Pacific, Guadalcanal was nicknamed Operation SHOESTRING, since the hastily mounted task force seemed barely adequate to fulfill its objective. The major Allied effort at this time was directed toward the North African campaign, which was given priority in resources. Moreover, the Japanese were experienced at jungle fighting. And despite the defeat at Midway, their naval strength surpassed that available to King.

Ironically, this imbalance contributed to the American ability to achieve the element of surprise. On August 7 a naval task force moved into the waters around the southern Solomons. As the American marines in transport ships caught their first glimpse of Guadalcanal through the morning mist, one of them echoed everyone's silent thought, "This place gives you the creeps." After bombarding the Japanese defenses, the marines landed and in full daylight occupied a narrow strip along the coast of Guadalcanal (as well as three small nearby islands), meeting only slight and scattered resistance. They then rushed in to capture the unfinished airfield, renaming it Henderson Field.

The ease of these landings was no indication of what lay ahead, for the battle over Guadalcanal would last six months. Recovering from their surprise over the American landings, the Japanese rushed a task force that attacked the smaller American fleet off the coast of Guadalcanal, inflicting extensive damage and sinking three heavy cruisers. The substantial American losses, in the words of naval historian Samuel Eliot Morison, constituted "probably the worst defeat ever inflicted on the United States navy in a fair fight." After the Japanese broke off the naval engagement, more American marines were landed on Guadalcanal. Although lacking adequate food and supplies, these men managed to hold their position. Meanwhile, the Japanese hurried additional reinforcements to their troops on

Guadalcanal through a line of supply the Americans referred to as the "Tokyo Express."

Ordered to hold the airstrip at any cost, the Americans got their first taste of jungle warfare. That battle, a "horrible nightmare to those who fought there," forced the Americans to pursue the Japanese into the jungle, where they seemingly blended into the background, hiding in underbrush or high in palm trees, as well as in caves and dugouts. At night Americans could not distinguish cries of animals from signal calls of the Japanese. While this fighting raged on the island, a series of naval battles continued in the seas around Guadalcanal. Morison, who witnessed the months of fighting, described the meaning of the conflict:

> Guadalcanal is not a name but an emotion, recalling desperate flights in the air, furious naval battles, frantic work at supplying and construction, savage fighting in the jungle, night broken by screaming bombs and deafening explosions of naval shells.

The decisive point in this prolonged struggle came on November 12–15 when the Americans — in the fifth and the largest of the series of the Guadalcanal naval battles — withstood a major Japanese thrust aimed at destroying the American position and landing more troops. The Japanese enjoyed numerical superiority in the ships committed to this battle, but the Americans took advantage of the quickness and maneuverability of their smaller ships. Thereafter, the Americans were able to reinforce their hold on Guadalcanal, while it was the Japanese who now suffered from the shortage of food and supplies. The fighting continued on land and sea until the first week of February 1943, when the Japanese withdrew some 11,000 troops. With the collapse of Japanese resistance, an elated American commander cabled: "Tokyo Express' no longer has terminus of Guadalcanal."

Thus, after six months of bitter warfare, Guadalcanal lay in American hands. The significance of the battle was immediately evident. As the struggle for the island shifted to American advantage following the naval confrontation, President Franklin D. Roosevelt observed, "It would seem that the turning point in this war has been reached," while Prime Minister Winston Churchill saw it as "the end of the beginning." Japan, however, attempted to construe the outcome as a victory. When the Japanese were finally evacuated, Radio Tokyo proclaimed that the object of restricting the Americans to a small part of Guadalcanal had been achieved, and Japan's troops were withdrawing to fight elsewhere. In fact, the Japanese recognized Guadalcanal as a major defeat. During the battle, a Japanese document emphasized that "the success or failure in recapturing Guadalcanal Island, and the vital naval battle related to it, is the fork in the road which leads to victory for them or for us." That assessment was correct.

The Island Campaign, 1943–1944

Indeed, Guadalcanal reversed the positions of the United States and Japan. Having failed in its offensives at Midway and in the Solomons, Japan fell back on a defensive strategy intended to hold its empire, the perimeter of which was reinforced with new airfields, munitions stockpiles, and strengthened garrisons. To secure the sea lanes vital to the integration of its holdings, Japan had to protect its shipping from American submarine attacks. In 1942 the United States sank more than 1 million tons of Japanese merchant shipping, more than Japanese shipyards could replace. Accordingly, the Japanese concentrated on accelerated production of aircraft carriers.

Success in halting the Japanese meant that the United States could begin offensive operations. There were now three routes by which the Americans could exert pressure on Japan: (1) entering the Asian mainland through China and Southeast Asia, (2) launching an island campaign northward from the base in Australia to the Philippines, or (3) mounting an island campaign through the western Pacific. The first route would have reinforced the Allied position in India, strengthened the Chinese army, and led to collaborating with the Chinese and the British to force the Japanese from China and Southeast Asia. This approach was favored by the British, who were determined to maintain their control of India and reestablish the European empires in Southeast Asia. The Australia-Philippines approach favored by MacArthur called for the use of the army, with naval support as necessary, to move on a land route over the large islands of New Guinea and the Philippines, thus forcing the Japanese from those areas and leading eventually to an invasion of Japan. The Pacific approach, which was advocated by King and Nimitz on behalf of the navy, involved the full utilization of naval power to capture a series of strategic islands in the Pacific. From those positions, it would be possible to disrupt Japanese sea lanes, bomb Japan itself, and blockade the Japanese islands.

Instead of selecting one approach, the United States chose all three, but the principal means of warfare — as reflected in the allocation of manpower and resources — was the Navy's Pacific island campaign. The reason for also adopting the other approaches had less to do with military strategy than with politics and rivalries among the Allies and the branches of the American armed services. It seemed impossible to ignore China and Southeast Asia, not only because of British interests but because of the claims that China made for assistance in its struggle against Japan. The Chinese cause, as noted, was popular in the United States; moreover, President Roosevelt sought to elevate China to major power status. For these reasons, it seemed imperative to bolster the Chinese army and national morale.

Lieutenant-General Joseph W. Stilwell, who was appointed chief-of-staff of the Chinese army in early 1942 as part of Chinese-American collaboration to strengthen Chinese resistance, undertook to restructure and modernize the Chinese military. Stilwell also supervised the construction of a land route of supply (the 478-mile-long Ledo Road) that originated in northern India, cut through the jungles, and crisscrossed the Himalayan Mountains to reach China. The American air force flew supplies to China by crossing the Himalayan Mountains in runs that became known as "flying the hump." These flights began in April 1942 after the Japanese had blocked land supply routes to China. Over the next forty-two months, the air force airlifted supplies to China on a daily basis. Flying over the Himalayas was extremely dangerous and made more difficult by a lack of reliable charts, an absence of radio navigation aids, and a dearth of reliable information about weather conditions. Nearly 600 aircraft were lost and 1,700 airmen were killed or missing during the "flying the hump" operation. Nonetheless, the airlift delivered approximately 650,000 tons of materiel vital to the Chinese war effort. In Burma, British and American guerilla units kept the Japanese off balance and prevented them from fully consolidating their position; by 1944, the Allies were able to begin offensive operations in that country.

The pursuit of both the MacArthur and naval strategies reflected the long-standing army-navy rivalry. Could Japan be defeated by the effective use of air and naval power? Or did that outcome require the defeat of the Japanese armies, including an invasion of Japan itself? Naval leaders assumed that the Pacific war could be fought and won on the sea; indeed a generation of American naval planning for a possible war with Japan had based strategy on that assumption. Combining air and naval operations to secure key islands would yield harbors and airfields from which strikes could be made against the next target. Eventually, the United States would be able to launch sustained bombing attacks against Japan. This use of air power supported by submarines controlling the seas around Japan would strangle the island nation.

This naval campaign was not intended to capture all Japanese-held islands. Some of the stronger positions would not be invaded; rather, those islands would be sealed off by air and sea power, rendering them useless to Japan. The extent to which American naval leadership pursued this plan for war in the Pacific was driven in part by the realization that the navy would be forced to play a subordinate role in the European conflict; if Europe were to be the "army's show," then the Pacific ought to be the "navy's show." MacArthur questioned whether the naval strategy would work, arguing that the projected island campaign would leave the navy and the air bases constructed on captured islands vulnerable to attack from the Japanese navy and air force. He preferred that the naval role be limited to protecting his New Guinea–Philippines campaign. Although MacArthur was able to continue his New Guinea operations, he was disappointed when Roosevelt and the Joint Chiefs of Staff authorized the naval operations proposed by Nimitz and King with the result that the United States began its "island-hopping" campaign across the western Pacific. This strategy followed classic military doctrine of concentrating strength against the enemy's strength: victory over Japan necessitated defeating the Imperial Navy in the Pacific.

This diversion of American resources in the Pacific war has been criticized by a number of scholars, including Henri Michel in his magisterial history of World War II. The early fighting in the Pacific demonstrated that the war against Japan would be fought and ultimately won on the ocean, Michel argues, but the "surprising thing was that the Americans took so long to draw the practical conclusions from this and assign tasks accordingly." Rather than coordinating air and sea power, strategy in the Pacific "bore the marks of a sort of compromise between two great feudal lords forcing their own rivalry on a nation under arms."

The island campaign was essential to the defeat of Japan. Underlying the navy's success was a massive buildup of the fleet. By 1944, the size of the American navy was many times greater than that of Japan. Like the Japanese, the Americans concentrated on carrier construction, but those produced by the United States were far superior in numbers and in size. For operations against Japanese-held islands, the navy organized task forces composed of warships, carriers, and landing craft whose advance would be preceded by land-based, long-range aircraft to provide cover. Making full use of the improved system of radar, these task forces were able to extend action over wide areas; their operations were meticulously planned and executed. While MacArthur moved slowly on New Guinea, the navy advanced thousands of miles against selected targets, always pushing relentlessly toward the heart of the Japanese Empire.

The island advance, begun in late 1943, brought repetition of the nightmarish warfare first experienced at Guadalcanal. Each attack began with naval and air bombardment of Japanese positions. Under cover of that barrage, the U.S. forces landed. It took many hours, sometimes days, to gain a secure foothold; until that point, the troops were vulnerable to attack from the Japanese defenders. Once established, the marines began to move into jungle, swamp, and often mountainous terrain. Every step they took risked death from a booby trap or a sniper's bullet. The Japanese dug into trenches, caves, and fortifications called "pill boxes" of hard logs, steel rails, and concrete. The pill boxes were located in patterns, so as troops advanced toward one, they would be caught in crossfire from another. Only shattering bombardment or hand-to-hand combat could force the Japanese from these fortifications.

The Americans won each of the battles for control of these small but strategic Pacific islands, but the victories were gained at considerable cost. The Japanese followed "the strategy of drawing blood," which made the Americans suffer heavy casualties. Moreover, given the nature of the warfare, medical facilities for the wounded were rudimentary. And neither side, as long as the battle was being waged, wanted to be burdened by taking prisoners. While American casualties were often high, they were consistently exceeded by those of the Japanese. This reversed the typical pattern in which invading forces are expected to absorb greater losses than are the defenders.

Heavy Japanese losses reflected a willingness, even an eagerness, to die for the emperor. The determination to fight to the last man, taking as many enemy lives as possible, characterized Japanese resistance. As their situation grew desperate, the Japanese often would gather in a group and advance in a wild Banzai suicide charge. Reporting on one such incident, an American officer observed: "We cornered fifty or so on the end of the island, where they attempted a Banzai charge. But we cut them down like overripe wheat, and they lay like tired children with their faces in the sand." The largest Banzai attack occurred on the island of Saipan, where more than three thousand Japanese—some with guns, some with bayonets, and others with no weapons—attacked two American battalions; they inflicted heavy casualties, but in the end all the attackers were killed. Besides the Banzai charges were numerous other suicides. Typically, the commander of forces on an island that was about to fall to the Americans would take his own life. In such a situation, the humiliated Japanese commander at Saipan issued a final message to his troops saying that he would die with them. Then, sitting on a rock facing Tokyo, the officer opened an artery with his sword and nodded to his adjutant, who shot him in the head. The other members of the commander's staff then committed suicide.

Within the year from October 1943 to October 1944, the island campaign yielded spectacular results. Americans established unquestioned naval predominance in the Pacific. The thrust began with the attack on the Gilbert Islands, which the Japanese had seized in early

1942; the critical battle in the Gilberts was on the island of Tarawa. In three days of intense combat, Americans absorbed heavy losses (1,100 killed and over 2,000 wounded) but secured control. As usual the Japanese defense was fanatical: 4,690 Japanese were killed, and only 17 soldiers survived to be taken prisoner.

The capture of the Gilberts provided a springboard for an attack on the Marshall Islands. The major strategic point in the Marshalls was the atoll of Kwajalein which, after another period of bitter fighting, was captured by the Americans in January 1944. In that battle 330 Americans were killed, while Japanese deaths totaled 8,500. From their positions in the Gilberts and the Marshalls, the Americans were able to encircle and bomb the large Japanese base at Truk in the Caroline Islands. In addition the Americans isolated another key Japanese base at Rabaul by air and sea attack. The Japanese still held Truk and Rabaul, but these islands held no strategic value.

The leadership in Tokyo recognized the implications of the American advance. As had characterized the strategy at Pearl Harbor and Midway, the Japanese again decided to gamble on victory over the Americans through one overwhelming naval achievement. Another large naval strike force was assembled and placed under the command of Vice-Admiral Jisaburo Ozawa. This force was deployed to protect the Marianas—"the absolute zone of national defense."

In mid-June 1944, the Americans landed troops on heavily fortified Saipan, one of three major strategic points in the Marianas believed by the Japanese to be impregnable. Tokyo cabled Ozawa that "the fate of the empire rests on this one battle." But by the time the battle began, the Japanese navy was no longer a match for the American fleet, which enjoyed numerical superiority in ships and aircraft. In addition, the American carriers and planes were more sophisticated, and the American pilots better trained. Altogether, the Americans and Japanese had from three- to four-times the ships and planes in the naval battle in the Marianas that they had thrown at one another at Midway two years earlier. But whereas the outcome of Midway had been a "miracle," the American victory in the Marianas was predictable. Nearly three hundred and fifty Japanese aircraft were shot down; in contrast, only twenty-three American planes were lost. The easily victorious American pilots and anti-aircraft gunners referred to the battle as "The Great Marianas Turkey Shoot."

Victory in the air and on the sea paved the way for the difficult conquest of the islands themselves. By early August the Americans had captured Saipan, Tinian, and Guam. The disparity in casualties continued to be striking—in the battles for those three islands, 5,000 Americans and 42,000 Japanese died. From bases in the Marianas, the American air force could easily attack the Japanese home islands; B-29 bombers, which had a range of 3,000 miles, were coming into service, and on October 12, the first B-29 bombing mission took off from Guam heading for Tokyo.

As the island campaign advanced, MacArthur's American and Australian forces gained control on New Guinea, and in October 1944 American troops landed in the Philippines. At the same time, in the battle of Leyte Gulf, the navy secured another decisive victory over the Japanese. This success assured American control of the sea and air around the Philippines and facilitated the liberation of those islands. The campaign in the Philippines, which extended over a period of ten months, enabled the United States to fulfill its promise to free the Filipinos. On a personal level, MacArthur returned in triumph, as promised. With the memories of the humiliating surrender still vivid in the nation's collective mind, the reestablishment of American control was an important accomplishment in terms of Philippine and American morale.

Yet the island campaign surpassed the significance of the New Guinea–Philippine campaign. It was the American naval predominance in the Pacific that led to the blockade of Japan and the bombing of its cities. It was through the control of the Gilberts, Marshalls, and Marianas that the navy opened the path leading directly to the Japanese home islands. By early 1945, the navy was prepared to capture two additional islands—Iwo Jima and Okinawa—which would be integral to the anticipated invasion of Japan itself.

Iwo Jima and Okinawa

A most compelling image of American forces in World War II was that captured by the famous photograph of a small group of American marines thrusting a flag atop Mount Suribachi on Iwo Jima. The gallantry evident in the photograph captured the essential quality of the American combat in the war against Japan. Widely reprinted in newspapers and magazines, the photograph taken by Joseph Rosenthal of the Associated Press later inspired a bronze statue erected just outside Washington, D.C. And the battles for Iwo Jima and Okinawa—the final two steps in the island campaign—indeed were the most monumental.

Iwo Jima is a barren volcanic island just eight miles square, but it was vital to both the Japanese and the Americans. Uninhabited except for the Japanese garrison, the island has beaches of volcanic ash and black cinders on which it is difficult to walk, virtually impossible to run. The northern part of the island features massive rocks and boulders and volcanic crevices. At the southern tip is the extinct volcano, Mount Suribachi, which rises 550 feet above sea level.

The importance of Iwo Jima lay in its location—750 miles from Tokyo, halfway between the Marianas and the Japanese home islands. For the Japanese, control of Iwo Jima was considered indispensable; from Iwo Jima, Tokyo could be warned of the approach of American aircraft, so its loss would increase the devastation of the bombing of the main islands. To the Americans, Iwo Jima provided a key refueling base for B-29 bombers (while the bombers could reach Japan from the Marianas, there was little margin for error, and if weather or enemy anti-aircraft fire forced the B-29s off course, they frequently were unable to return) as well as a base for fighter planes to accompany them. (Fighter planes lacked the fuel capacity to fly the entire Marianas-Japan-Marianas route.)

The battle for Iwo Jima proved to be one of the bloodiest of the entire war. To some extent the great cost in human lives resulted from the American failure to maintain the momentum of the island campaign. Naval historian Morison argued that "[W]e could have walked into Iwo in September [1944], right after securing the Marianas." Instead, the Joint Chiefs of Staff debated the next step in the Pacific war with the result that naval power was diverted toward the Philippine campaign. Time spent waging the Battle of Leyte Gulf and supporting the Philippine landings gave the Japanese the opportunity to reinforce their position on Iwo Jima. By early 1945 the Japanese had a force of 23,000 men there, and had transformed the island into a fortress with an elaborate cave-and-tunnel network protected by thick walls of volcanic ash and cement. From any of three airfields on the island, planes could lift to attack invaders.

In preparation for the invasion scheduled for February 1945, the United States Air Force and Navy carried out the "most prolonged and most disappointing" bombardment of any Pacific island. The bombing of Iwo Jima began in August 1944, after the Marianas had been secured, and was increased to a daily barrage after December. But the bombardments had negligible effect on Japan's defenses. When marines were landed on February 19, they encountered fire from the well-protected Japanese positions. Ankle deep in the loose volcanic ash, the Americans had to fight yard by yard against a well-trained and well-positioned enemy. Slowly, the Americans, with their flame throwers, bazookas, and grenades, overcame Japanese resistance. "The fighting," in the words of the commander of the marines in the Pacific, "was the toughest the Marines ran across in 168 years." On just the first day, American casualties totaled 2,500 of the 30,000 men who had landed. By day and night the battle raged over all parts of the island. The vital point was Mount Suribachi, from which the Japanese shelled the beaches and advancing troops. After intense and prolonged fighting, the Americans captured Suribachi on February 23. Three weeks later the Americans had "secured" Iwo Jima, although warfare continued against pockets of resistance for several more weeks.

The cost on both sides was great. In their futile effort to hold this tiny island, more than 22,000 Japanese gave their lives. Only about 1,000 Japanese were taken prisoner, most of those during the mopping-up operation. To secure Iwo Jima, nearly 8,000 American sailors and marines lost their lives and 20,000 were wounded.

The capture of Iwo Jima secured America's strategic predominance. The air bases, now in American hands, enabled the air force to intensify the bombing of Japan's military and industrial centers.

But even the heavy losses on Iwo Jima were surpassed by those in the final great island battle of the campaign, that for Okinawa. Now the Japanese were more determined than ever, even fanatical, for Okinawa is just 365 miles southwest of the main Japanese island of Kyushu. Okinawa is the largest of the Ryukyu chain of islands, which have been part of Japan since 1879. It is also larger and more heavily populated than the other islands on which the Americans and the Japanese had been fighting since 1942. About seventy miles long and from three to twenty-three miles wide, Okinawa was home to about half a million people, mostly engaged in farming.

Recognizing the importance of this island, the Japanese had fortified it, again following the in-depth defense tactics used on Iwo Jima. About 100,000 troops were entrenched in interconnecting tunnels and caves, as well as in pill boxes. On Okinawa, fighting to the last man, which had been characteristic of Japanese resistance throughout the long island campaign beginning with Guadalcanal, was even more pronounced. Indeed, suicide became part of national policy. Whereas earlier there had been some Banzai charges and kamikaze raids, the frenzy to repel the American advance at Okinawa included massive use of the kamikaze tactic.

For the United States, Okinawa was considered essential as a staging area for the anticipated invasion of the main Japanese islands. Moreover, the capture of Okinawa would isolate Japan from China and Southeast Asia, and the control of the several airfields on the island would shorten American bombing routes.

After ten days of bombardment by sea and air, American troops landed on Okinawa on April 1, 1945. Initially, the Japanese offered little resistance, and the Americans easily occupied the northern three-fourths of the island. But the early going proved to be deceptive, for the Japanese abruptly challenged the Americans in the waters around Okinawa and then engaged them in battle on the island.

Beginning on April 6, the Japanese launched large-scale kamikaze warfare against the American fleet in the waters off Okinawa. The Kamikaze Corps was organized in response to the American domination of the air and sea. American attacks had largely eliminated the air groups of the Japanese Imperial Navy, and the fleet itself had been decimated. The kamikaze campaign was intended to immobilize the American navy, especially the carriers, in a desperate effort to protect the homeland from invasion. For its kamikaze warfare, Japan was able to use obsolete aircraft and undertrained pilots; indeed many of the suicide flyers were quite young and had little, if any, combat experience. Ideally, the kamikaze pilot would fly his plane directly into an enemy ship. A bomb mounted in the nose of the aircraft would explode on impact.

Kamikaze pilots were volunteers who willingly sacrificed their lives for the homeland. Typically, before departing on such missions, pilots would toast the emperor and the glorious death awaiting them. They would then be locked into the cockpits of their aircraft to take off on their last earthly mission. The kamikaze campaign drew upon Japan's veneration of the emperor, loyalty to country and superiors, and belief in the life of the spirit after death. The word *kamikaze*, which means "heavenly wind," was derived from a moment of historical importance. In 1570 the Japanese had been saved from a Chinese invasion by a fortuitous typhoon that blew the enemy fleet out to sea; just as that "heavenly wind" had saved Japan earlier, so the kamikaze would save the nation in another hour of peril.

Kamikaze warfare was practiced in two ways: individual pilots acted independently, or groups of pilots flew successive waves of suicide attacks (*kikusui*) against selected targets. The latter tactic was, of course, the more lethal, and was usually accompanied by the deployment of conventional aircraft to draw enemy planes away from the ships under attack.

For men aboard ship under kamikaze attack, the only defense was to fire antiaircraft guns with the hope of downing the assaulting airplane before it (or they) reached the ship. During these attacks, it was virtually impossible to tend to the injured or put out fires. In the first kikusui attack off Okinawa on April 6–7, the Japanese committed 355 kamikazes who inflicted heavy losses. An eyewitness to an attack told the following story:

> Then it was that a man aboard our ship caught the first glimpse of three enemy planes. . . . [B]efore a half a dozen shots could be fired from the [carrier] *Bunker Hill*, the first kamikaze had dropped his 550-pound bomb on the ship and plunged his plane squarely into her 34 waiting planes in a shower of burning gasoline. . . . Some of the pilots were blown overboard by the explosion. . . . But before a move could be made to fight the flames, another kamikaze came whining out of the clouds, straight into the deadly antiaircraft guns of the ship. . . . A five-inch shell that should have set him afire

riddled his plane with metal. But still he came. Passing over the stern of the ship he dropped his bomb right in the middle of the blazing planes. Then he flipped over and torched through the flight deck. . . . That was the end of the attack and beginning of the fight for survival. The entire rear end of the ship by this time was burning with uncontrollable fury.

The kamikaze tactics continued throughout April and May; some 3,000 sacrificial flights were launched. Twenty-one ships were sunk and 67 were damaged; Allied naval casualties totaled 5,000 men killed and an equal number wounded.

Kamikaze warfare proved to be Japan's most effective means of countering American naval supremacy. Continued in greater concentration, the kamikaze tactic might have forced the United States to revise its strategy. But the Japanese were incapable of sustaining the level of kamikaze warfare waged with such lethal effectiveness around Okinawa. The American navy was staggered by the onslaught, but it remained intact and able to proceed toward Japan.

In addition to the kamikaze tactic, the Japanese, in another desperate move, committed the remnants of their once-dominant navy to the defense of Okinawa. They managed to assemble one cruiser, eight destroyers, and the large battleship *Yamato*, but they no longer had any carriers, so the fleet was deprived of air support. This entire (and final) use of naval power was, in essence, a kamikaze mission; the *Yamato* and its covering squadron were sent against a numerically superior enemy to cause as much damage as possible, but they were not expected to return—the ships had only enough fuel to reach Okinawa. The confrontation was brief and decisive. American fighters and bombers took to the air and attacked; *Yamato*, the cruiser, and four destroyers went down. The Japanese navy had made its last stand.

The mentality evident in the kamikaze and naval operations characterized the defense of Okinawa. After allowing the Americans to become established on the greater part of the island, the Japanese bitterly defended their strongholds. It was a repetition of Iwo Jima. The Americans advanced yard by yard. Only tanks, flame throwers, or explosive charges forced the Japanese from their caves, tunnels, and pill boxes. Thousands of Japanese were burned alive or suffocated. It took two months of furious fighting before the Americans were able to secure Okinawa. The Japanese fought almost to the last man. As their fate became inevitable, there were banzai charges and suicides of officers. Okinawa was the costliest battle of the Pacific war. In the fighting on the island, 12,500 Americans were killed and 36,000 wounded. The nature of the Japanese resistance was underscored by their losses: more than 110,000 men killed, just 7,800 taken prisoner.

Japan, 1945: The Refusal to Surrender

By early 1945 Japan was a defeated nation. The Americans had reached the threshold of the main islands. The series of defeats beginning with Midway and ending with Okinawa had not only cracked Japan's defenses, but also decimated its navy and air force. Japan was defenseless. Relentless "fire bombings" brought an especially lethal death from the skies. Intended to destroy urban areas as well as civilian morale, these nighttime raids attacked densely populated sections of cities and their easily inflammable residences. Low-flying B-29s (by flying low they could carry more payload and bomb more precisely) dropped tons of bombs that raised intense heat and fire, causing violent and uncontrollable storms of air currents. Areas hit by the firebombing raids were left awash in a sea of flames.

The first firebombing hit Tokyo on March 9–10, 1945; in it 334 B-29 bombers dropped 2,000 tons of bombs on a densely populated section of the city. Raging fires destroyed a quarter of a million buildings. One million persons were left homeless, and about 90,000 persons were killed. "In the black Sumida River," an army surgeon wrote, "countless bodies were floating, clothed bodies, naked bodies, all as black as charcoal. It was unreal. These were dead people, but you couldn't tell whether they were men or women. You couldn't even tell if the objects floating by were arms and legs or pieces of burnt wood." The Tokyo firebombing was, in the words of historian Russell Buchanan, "one of the worst holocausts of all time." Similar raids against other cities and daily conventional bombing attacks reduced most of Japan's major cities to rubble.

Not only did the Americans control the air, but they also dominated the waters around Japan. A naval blockade made it impossible for Japan to receive raw materials. The Japanese merchant marine, which had once dominated the sea lanes of Asia, had been reduced by air and submarine attacks to one-tenth its prewar size. Steel production in Japan was at one-fourth its 1941 level. Everywhere, especially in the large cities, food was in short supply. By any rational standard, Japan's prospects were hopeless.

Why did Japan not surrender? Why did its leaders continue a war that could bring only greater suffering and destruction to the Japanese people? The ultranationalists, especially in the military, refused to accept the evidence of defeat and believed that Japan could still be saved. In a classic example of "wishful thinking," they claimed that the army in the main islands would be able to resist an American invasion and enable Japan to negotiate a compromise peace. The ultranationalists also assumed that the Soviet Union, with which Japan had entered into a nonaggression pact in 1941 and which had not yet become involved in the war in the Pacific, would be of some assistance. Just as Japan had not attacked Russia when it was reeling under the German advance in 1941–42, so perhaps the Soviets would not take advantage of Japan in its hour of peril. Assuming that Soviet and American differences would surface, the ultranationalists believed that the Soviets might seek the preservation of Japanese power to counter that of the United States in the Pacific.

Also, the movement to end the war—if it were to be effective—required strong leadership, a quality conspicuously lacking in Japanese politics. A peace faction, comprised of several of the leaders who had been repudiated in 1941 for their failure to follow the ultranationalists as they pressed for war, had been reemerging since 1943 and looked to the emperor for guidance and support. While evidently sympathetic with the peace movement, Emperor Hirohito declined to abandon the passive role imposed on his office by the constitution. The most outspoken advocate of an early end to the war was former premier Prince Fumimaro Konoye; in early 1945 Konoye, who as premier in 1940–41 had worked desperately but futilely to avoid war with the United States, wrote to the emperor that defeat had to be accepted and the war ended immediately. Japan's defeats of 1944–45 brought more moderate, but not more decisive, leadership to the key office of premier. General Hideki Tojo resigned as a consequence of the defeats in the Marianas, but his successor, General Kuniaki Koiso, was caught between the advocates of ending the war and the ultranationalists who urged its continuation. With the invasion of Okinawa, Koiso resigned and was replaced by the eighty-year-old Admiral Kantaro Suzuki. The old admiral sought peace, but he pressed for terms other than "unconditional surrender" and endeavored, without success, to use the Soviet Union as a mediator.

Rather than facing reality and saving many lives, the Japanese leaders remained preoccupied with placating various internal factions, while desperately hoping for outside support. Japan's lack of responsible, far-sighted leadership meant that its people suffered needless losses. Only the devastating power of the atomic bomb—with its many and ominous implications for the postwar world—would finally end the war.

USS *West Virginia* engulfed in flames after the surprise aerial attack of Pearl Harbor by the Japanese, December 7, 1941. *(80 G 19917)*

Prisoners with their hands tied behind their backs on "The Bataan Death March," May 1942. *(127-N-114541)*

Unless otherwise noted, all photographs are courtesy of the National Archives, Washington, D.C.

Crammed with men
and material for the
invasion, this Coast
Guard-manned LST
nears the Japanese-
held shore.
Cape Gloucester,
New Britain,
December 24, 1943.
(26-G-3056)

Pilots pleased over their victory during the Marshall Islands attack
grin across the tail of an F6F Hellcat on board the USS *Lexington*
after shooting down 17 out of 20 Japanese planes heading for Tarawa,
November 1943. *(80-G-470985)*

U.S. Marine 'Raiders' and their dogs, used for scouting and running messages, head off for the jungle front lines in Bougainville, Solomon Islands. *(84-68407)*

American troops storm a North African beach from a Coast Guard–manned "seahorse" landing craft during final amphibious maneuvers, 1944. *(26-G-2326)*

240 mm Howitzer of Battery 'B', 697th Field Artillery Battalion just before firing into German-held territory, around Mignano, Italy, April 1944. *(111-SC-187126)*

Japanese plane shot down as it attempted a Kamikaze attack on the USS *Kitkun Bay*, near the Mariana Islands, June 1944. *(80-G-238363)*

Crewmembers of the USS *South Dakota* attend a service held in honor of shipmates killed in the air action off Guam, June 19, 1944. *(80-G-238322)*

American troops in a tank passing the Arc de Triomphe following the liberation of Paris, August 1944. *(208-YE-68)*

Below: With a canvas tarpaulin for a church and packing cases for an altar, a Navy chaplain holds Mass for fallen Marines at Saipan. Photo by Sgt. Steele, June 1944. *(127-N-82262)*

Nurses of a field hospital who arrived in France via England and Egypt after three years of service, August 12, 1944. *(112-SGA-44-10842)*

General MacArthur surveys the beachhead on Leyte Island, soon after American forces swept ashore from a gigantic liberation armada into the central Philippines, making good on his promise, "I shall return." *(26-G-3584)*

An American roadblock is set up with 30-caliber heavy machine guns, and a tank detroyer is ready for action on Adolph Hitler Strasse. 1st Battalion, 157th Regiment, 45th Division, December 10, 1944. *U.S. Army Center of Military History (SC364301)*

Prime Minister Winston S. Churchill, President Franklin D. Roosevelt, and Premier Josef Stalin at the Yalta Conference, where they made final plans for the defeat of Germany, February 1945. *(111-SC-260486)*

American soldiers walk among emaciated survivors along a road in the
Ebensee concentration camp. May 8, 1945. Ebensee, Austria. *Credit: United
States Holocaust Memorial Museum, courtesy of Bert Weston (09848)*

Pilots aboard a U.S. Navy aircraft carrier receive last-minute instructions before taking off to attack industrial and military installations in Tokyo. February 17, 1945. *(208-N-38374)*

Debilitated by Japanese fire and the treacherous black-ash sands of Iwo Jima, dozens of military vehicles lay immobilized on the small, volcanic fortress. *Photo: Robert M. Warren, ca. February/March 1945. (26-G-4474)*

The "Little Boy" mushroom cloud as seen from one of three
Boeing B-29s that accompanied the Superfortress Bomber,
Enola Gay. Forty-three seconds after the 9,700-pound bomb was
released, the cloud rose to 1,900 feet above the city of Hiroshima,
August 6, 1945. *Credit: United States Air Force*

A dense column of smoke rises more than 60,000 feet into the air over the Japanese port of Nagasaki. "Fat Man," the second atomic bomb ever used in warfare, was dropped on the industrial center August 8, 1945, from a U. S. B-29 Superfortress. Together the bombs dropped by the U.S. on Nagasaki and Hiroshima killed between 150,000 and 220,000 people immediately (not including long-term mortality). *(208-N-43888)*

CHAPTER FIVE

The Diplomatic Front: Roosevelt and the American Vision of the Postwar World

"War," the German military theoretician Karl von Clausewitz wrote in the early nineteenth century, "is nothing but a continuation of politics by different means." As that often-cited quotation underscores, a nation engages in war not as an end in itself, but to achieve political objectives. Beyond the essential objective of destroying the military power of the Axis, the United States fought World War II to change the international system in ways that would foster a stable world.

The strength of the enemy necessitated the military alliance with Great Britain, the Soviet Union, China, and the other Allied nations. Each of the other powers brought their own long-term objectives into the alliance. In the Declaration of the United Nations, which was signed on January 1, 1942, the members of the Allied Coalition agreed on their common purpose of defeating the Axis powers and creating a postwar world based on the principles of political freedom, economic cooperation, self-determination, and disarmament. Eventually, forty-seven nations adhered to the Declaration of the United Nations. Yet beyond that fundamental agreement, the Allied powers, especially in the relationship among the Big Three, differed over military strategy and the postwar settlement. The United States, Great Britain, and the Soviet Union each brought into the alliance immediate and long-term objectives reflecting their histories, traditions, ideologies, and wartime experiences. The relationship among the major powers revealed constant points of difference, but in that respect, the World War II Allies were by no means unique. Writing in the late eighteenth century, the French diplomat, Comte de Segur, observed that military alliances were "marriages followed promptly by divorce . . . a common enemy momentarily unites, a constant jealousy separates."

President Franklin D. Roosevelt set forth the American postwar objectives. Contrary to the advice of Comte de Segur, he envisioned the preservation of the wartime alliance in a world of increased international cooperation and interdependence. It blended a traditional reliance on power politics with the idealism of the Atlantic Charter. The nations that fought together against the Axis were to cooperate in the preservation of international peace. To Roosevelt the "constant jealousy," or points of divergence among the Allies, had to be reconciled so that this alliance would not be a "marriage followed promptly by divorce." Roosevelt's postwar objectives, broadly stated, can be summarized as envisioning: (1) a strong American role in international affairs, symbolized by leadership in the United Nations; (2) Soviet-American cooperation to help preserve peace; (3) China's emergence as a major force for peace in Asia; (4) the gradual demise of colonial empires, leading to independent states in Asia and Africa.

A "strong" president who had provided decisive leadership on domestic issues and foreign policy, Roosevelt, in the midst of a global war, became an even more dominant figure. Distrustful of the State Department and disdainful of Cordell Hull, who served as secretary of state until late 1944, Roosevelt relied on his own instincts, a few close advisers, and a variety of special emissaries to help him define and implement the major elements of his foreign policy. While Roosevelt frequently ignored the State Department, its leadership and the nation's foreign policy elite generally shared his vision of the postwar world. The war generated an enormous number of books and studies on how postwar peace could be preserved, and in large part their recommendations paralleled Roosevelt's objectives.

Roosevelt worked diligently to preserve the inherently fragile wartime coalition and to achieve his postwar goals. He corresponded frequently with British prime minister Winston Churchill and soviet premier Josef Stalin. In addition, he met on several occasions with Churchill and twice undertook long trips to meet with both Churchill and Stalin. At the first Big Three Conference held at Teheran, Iran, in November 1943, an expectant and buoyant atmosphere prevailed because the Allies had gained the military ascendancy in Europe and in the Pacific. At the conference, the British and Americans finally promised to launch the cross-Channel invasion of German-occupied France the following spring, thus satisfying the long-standing Russian demand for a "second front" in Western Europe. For his part, Stalin reaffirmed that following the defeat of Germany, the Soviet Union would help the United States in the struggle against Japan. Beyond those military agreements, the Teheran Conference provided an opportunity for discussing postwar plans in a candid and forthright manner. Altogether, the conference led to much optimism that the Big Three would work together in the postwar world. By the time of the second Big Three Conference, which was held at Yalta in the Soviet Union in February 1945, Germany was on the verge of defeat and differences had already developed between Russia and the Western Allies over the postwar status of Eastern Europe and the treatment of Germany. Circumstances required compromise which, Roosevelt believed, would help assure the Soviet Union's postwar cooperation.

Although Roosevelt's wartime diplomacy was criticized by some contemporaries and scholars as naive, Roosevelt was truly a realist. A thoughtful, calculating, well-informed leader, his objectives were grounded in his nation's interests and the potential, as well as the limits, of its power. Championing the United Nations, international cooperation, and self-determination of peoples were not, as some critics alleged, expressions of an ill-founded idealism, but rather were objectives that blended idealism with realism. Roosevelt himself summarized the character of his leadership when he wrote that "I dream dreams, but am, at the same time, an intensely practical person." Roosevelt the "practical idealist" can be seen in the ways in which he endeavored to realize his four major objectives.

The United Nations

Roosevelt's overriding fear was that the United States would retreat, as it had following World War I, from substantial responsibility for preserving world peace. To assure that Americans would assume an enlarged role in world affairs, Roosevelt cultivated popular support for a new international organization to replace the discredited League of Nations. The American public responded enthusiastically to this movement, which was championed by various groups and both major political parties. To the vast majority of Americans, membership in this new organization provided a "second chance" for the nation to show its commitment to the preservation of world peace. The nation's failure to join the League of Nations after World War I, it was widely believed, had contributed to the international instability that led to World War II. The "lesson" was clear: that "mistake" could not be repeated. A popular motion picture, *Wilson*, reinforced the point as it portrayed the World War I president who had fought for the League of Nations as a noble prophet whose dream had been undermined by narrow-minded senators who rejected the Treaty of Versailles and U.S. membership in the League. In a significant move, Congress in 1943 passed a resolution promising support for a world peacekeeping organization; this signaled that partisanship would not again prevent the nation from providing international leadership. By early 1945, fully 90 percent of the American public favored inclusion in a world body. Eight out of ten Americans approved the use of force by the new organization in order to keep the peace. Though the conference at San Francisco that formally established the United Nations met after his death, Roosevelt had provided the essential leadership in assuring the American commitment to the new international body.

Roosevelt diverged from the public view of the United Nations on one important point. Most Americans assumed that the new organization would be based on the equality of nations, and that all members would participate in the preservation of international peace. They foresaw an organization which, like its predecessor the League of Nations, would rely on a system of collective security whereby all members would cooperate, economically and militarily, against aggressive nations. This idealistic vision had much appeal,

for Americans tended to abhor suggestions of reliance on such concepts as the balance of power and spheres of influence, since those
practices accepted the inequality of nations and seemed to have
led to conflict in the past. Roosevelt appeared to share such views;
indeed, when he addressed Congress after the Yalta Conference, he
spoke of a postwar world free of power politics:

> [The war] ought to spell the end of the system of unilateral action,
> the exclusive alliances, the spheres of influence, the balances of
> power, and all the other expedients that have been tried for cen-
> turies—and have always failed. We propose to substitute for all
> these, a universal organization in which all peace-loving nations
> will finally have a chance to join.

Roosevelt actually believed that international stability could only
be achieved by the strength of, and cooperation among, the major
powers; he considered collective security to be impractical, as the
history of the League of Nations underscored. Beginning early in
the war, he spoke privately of the "four policemen"—the United
States, the Soviet Union, Great Britain, and China—as principally
responsible for the preservation of postwar peace. Each "policeman"
was to be dominant in its area of the world (sphere of influence).
As circumstances required, the four would cooperate to preserve
international stability.

Roosevelt's concept of the postwar world assumed not the end,
but the continuation of power politics. As the plans for the United
Nations progressed, Roosevelt's four-policemen concept took form
in the U.N. Security Council; its permanent members (the "four
policemen" plus France) were to be principally responsible for
international peace. "Though the Four Policemen disappeared in
substance," historian Robert Divine observes, "the grant of veto
power to the permanent members of the Security Council continued
Roosevelt's insistence on great-power control over the enforcement
of peace."

How can Roosevelt's public promotion of a United Nations
based on collective security and his personal commitment to big-
power domination be reconciled? His support of the United Nations
rested on the belief that it was necessary to involve the United States
permanently in world affairs. Big-power control, historian Robert

Dallek writes, was "obscure[d] . . . through a United Nations organization which would satisfy widespread demand in the United States for new idealistic or universalist arrangements for assuring the peace." Hence, Roosevelt's championing of membership in the United Nations, capitalizing on popular enthusiasm, was vital to securing public support for American involvement in world affairs.

American leaders believed that besides the stabilizing effect of the United Nations, the preservation of international order required greater economic cooperation. An "open world" of low trade barriers and the flow of investment capital, it was widely assumed, enhanced interdependence and reduced the prospects of war. U.S. officials also recognized that at war's end, America would be the dominant industrial and financial power in a world of devastated economies and societies; international recovery and reestablishment of trade required new initiatives. So the United States took the leadership. It invited some 1,300 delegates from forty-four nations to the United Nations Monetary and Financial Conference, held at Bretton Woods, New Hampshire, in July 1944. The Bretton Woods Conference led to the establishment of the International Monetary Fund and the International Bank for Reconstruction and Development (commonly called the World Bank). Dominated by the United States, these organizations sought to ensure a postwar capitalist world by reestablishing financial stability and international trade based on gold and the U.S. dollar.

To achieve postwar political and economic stability, Roosevelt considered it essential to incorporate the other major allies into the new system. Cooperation with Britain was taken for granted, but building an enduring partnership with the Soviet Union and addressing the internal problems that threatened China's great-power status presented substantial challenges and received much of the president's attention.

Soviet-American Cooperation

Among Roosevelt's most monumental challenges was the promotion of long-term Soviet-American cooperation. The mutual need to defeat Hitler created the "strange alliance" between the world's preeminent capitalist and communist nations. The Soviet and American governments had long distrusted one another; in Moscow, leaders recalled the Western hostility toward the communist revolution of 1917 and the prolonged period of American non-recognition of the Soviet government (not until 1934 did the United States extend diplomatic recognition). In Washington, officials could not ignore many unsavory aspects of Soviet rule: the efforts to promote communist revolutions internationally; the totalitarian character of the Soviet government, which had been vividly evident during the brutal purges of Stalin's political opponents in the late 1930s; Stalin's deal with the Germans (the Nazi-Soviet Non-Aggression Pact of August 1939) which facilitated Hitler's invasion of Poland and enabled the parallel Russian takeover of the Baltic states and its aggression against Finland.

Roosevelt shared the nation's disgust over much of what had occurred in Russia since 1917, but circumstances forced cooperation. "I can't take communism," he once wrote, "but to cross this bridge I would hold hands with the Devil." To build cooperation Roosevelt relied heavily on personal diplomacy, believing that through discussions and negotiations directly with Stalin, the Americans and Soviets could reach certain understandings. Following their first meeting at the Teheran Conference, Roosevelt reported that he had found in Stalin a man "something like me . . . a realist."

Roosevelt's aspirations for Soviet-American friendship found wide support among the American public. In a dramatic reversal of prewar sentiments, Americans came to look very favorably upon the Russian people and even the dictatorial government of Josef Stalin. Americans admired the dogged Russian resistance to the German invasion and appreciated in particular the rigors of the Battle of Stalingrad. When they were asked to characterize the Russian people by selecting from a list of twenty-five adjectives, Americans responded "hardworking" (61 percent) and "brave" (48 percent); few persons associated negative attributes with the Russians. On several occasions when public opinion polls asked which nation—Britain, China, the United States, or the Soviet Union—was contributing the most to winning the war, Americans always ranked either their own country or the Soviet Union first and the other second, and, in all cases, both were seen as contributing far more than Britain or China. Respect for the Soviet contribution was especially strong during the critical winter of 1942–43 when Americans, despite their own offensives in North Africa and the Pacific, rallied around the Russians fighting the Battle of Stalingrad. Popular interest in that struggle has been described by historian Ralph Levering:

> This, it was sensed even then, was the crucial battle of the war, and millions of attentive Americans followed the shifting tides in the streets of the city and on the Volga plain as they would now follow a "crucial" televised football game. The hesitant American advances on small Pacific islands were as nothing compared with the epic quality of this struggle.

When the American public was asked in 1943 what people, not armies, were working hardest to win the war, they placed the Russians first (48 percent), themselves next (26 percent) and the British a distant third (13 percent). The press, radio, and film industry reinforced these attitudes by consistently portraying the Soviet Union in positive terms. Several popular movies dramatized the fighting on the Eastern Front. The book *Mission to Moscow*, written by former Russian ambassador Joseph Davies, and the film based on it presented Soviet leaders as men of honesty and integrity. Wendell Willkie, the Republican candidate for president in 1940, wrote the best-selling *One World*, which spoke glowingly of Stalin and other Soviet leaders, as well as of the economic and social progress the Russian people had made under their communist government. *Life* and *Time* magazines—the most influential journals of the era—extolled Russian virtues. *Time* named Stalin its "Man of the Year" in 1943. A special issue of *Life*, featuring a smiling Stalin on the cover, was devoted entirely to the Soviet Union. From the several pro-Russian articles and pages of photographs, Americans learned that Vladimir Lenin, the leader of the communist revolution of 1917, was "perhaps the greatest man of modern times" and that Stalin and his fellow leaders were "tough, loyal, capable administrators . . . 'Men of Good Will.'" *Life* concluded that the Russians were "one hell of a people [who] look like Americans, dress like Americans, and think like Americans."

This identification with the Russians encouraged Americans to believe that the wartime alliance would lead to postwar cooperation. Repeatedly, public opinion polls revealed confidence that the Russians could be trusted after the war. As a result, Roosevelt enjoyed strong popular backing for his efforts to build Soviet-American cooperation.

Roosevelt assumed that he and his fellow realist, Stalin, could resolve their differences. And to a large extent they succeeded in so doing. Perhaps the most vexing issue, however, was the future status of Eastern Europe. The Soviets sought recognition of their dominance over that region which twice within the previous thirty years had been the path for devastating German invasions of their homeland. Soviet security, Stalin reiterated in messages to British and American officials, demanded "friendly" governments along Russia's western borders. For the British and Americans, such claims posed problems. The British had gone to war in 1939 to uphold Polish sovereignty; they were not prepared to see German control replaced by that of the Soviet Union. London was the headquarters of the Polish government-in-exile that had fled Warsaw at the time of the German invasion in 1939. Both the British and American governments, as well as public opinion in those countries, held to the ideal of the self-determination of peoples. In the Atlantic Charter, Roosevelt and Churchill had pledged to oppose "territorial changes that do not accord with the freely expressed wishes of the peoples concerned" and "to have sovereign rights and self-government restored to those who have been forcibly deprived of them."

Yet Roosevelt recognized that increased Soviet influence in Eastern Europe could not be denied; indeed, he assumed that the Russians would function as the "policeman" of that area. The question confronting the president was how to reconcile Russian influence with the concept of self-determination. Roosevelt delayed forthright negotiations on Eastern Europe—especially the thorny subject of Poland—and permitted military developments to resolve the issues. Thus Roosevelt, in meetings with Stalin at the Teheran Conference, tacitly acknowledged Russian demands as reasonable, but urged that the Eastern European question be handled by the Russians in ways that would not alienate world opinion. He pointedly observed that 6 to 7 million American voters were of Polish descent and that he could not risk losing their support by appearing to sanction the loss of their ancestral homeland's sovereignty.

By the time of the Big Three meeting at Yalta, the future of Poland had been substantially determined. In early 1944, Russian armies crossed into Polish territory and, as they pushed the Germans to the west, established a provisional government headed by Polish communists and headquartered at Lublin. This Committee of National Liberation became the vehicle for establishing Russian control over Poland. The British and the Polish government-in-exile protested, but to no avail. Hence, when the Polish question was discussed at the Yalta Conference, Churchill and Roosevelt faced the fact of a Poland with a functioning pro-Soviet government supported by the Russian army. Meeting with congressional leaders prior to his departure to Yalta, Roosevelt forthrightly acknowledged that spheres of influence were a reality the United States had to accept; he observed "that the Russians had the power in Eastern Europe, that it was obviously impossible to have a break with them and that, therefore, the only practicable course was to use what influence we had to ameliorate the situation."

At the Yalta Conference, Roosevelt gained a compromise. Stalin agreed to the broadening of the Lublin government to include representatives of the government-in-exile and other important groups, and to the holding of timely free and democratic elections. As for the remainder of Eastern Europe (where Russian armies by that time were also well entrenched), the Big Three agreed to the Declaration on Liberated Europe. Like the Polish settlement, the declaration provided for participation of all political groups in provisional governments to be followed by free, democratic elections. While the agreements failed to provide any international guarantees for their implementation, they did, at least, place some moral obligation on the Soviet Union to act with restraint. "For all intents and purposes," Dallek concludes, "[Roosevelt] conceded that Eastern Europe was a Soviet sphere of influence." Clearly, Roosevelt regarded that concession as inevitable, given the Soviet's military position and security concerns and the need for continued cooperation. The settlements on Eastern Europe were, simply, the best he could get. "Roosevelt's chief concern," historian John Lewis Gaddis maintains, "was cosmetic: to put the best possible face on a bad situation in order to make palatable to the American public the postwar expansion of Soviet influence."

Moreover, Roosevelt's acquiescence in Soviet domination of Eastern Europe was made within the atmosphere of give-and-take on a number of questions, which included Soviet concessions to the interests of the United States on other issues. At Yalta, Stalin promised to enter the war against Japan within three months of the end of the conflict in Europe. To Americans who anticipated that an invasion of the main Japanese islands would result in substantial casualties, Russian support in the final campaign against the Japanese was a high priority. Also, the Soviet leader accepted the American plans for the new international organization.

Although Roosevelt worked throughout the war to reach certain understandings with the Soviet Union, his actions were not naive. A degree of skepticism regarding the Russians was evident in his decision to withhold information about the top-secret development of the atomic bomb. Roosevelt did enter into secret confidences with Churchill about full postwar Anglo-American coordination in the development of atomic energy for military and commercial purposes. Excluding the Soviet Union from such information (its agents in the United States were aware of the bomb project) was hardly reassuring to Russian leaders. Regardless of the reasons for concealing the development of the atomic bomb, Roosevelt recognized the difficulties of working with the Soviet Union. As disagreements continued after the Yalta Conference, an exasperated Roosevelt privately exclaimed, "we can't do business with Stalin." Yet in his last message to Churchill, he wrote of the importance of continuing efforts to work together: "I would minimize the general Soviet problem as much as possible. . . . Most of [the problems] straighten out. . . . We must be firm, however, and our course thus far is correct."

China's International Status

Roosevelt was committed to assisting China in assuming a prominent role in postwar Asia. The defeat of Japan would leave a power
vacuum that a resurgent China, friendly with the United States and
one of the "four policemen," would help to fill. To raise China's
international status during the war, the United States ended its
long-standing, unequal treaty relationship with China and its policy
of excluding Chinese immigrants. More important, Roosevelt insisted on treating China as a power equal to the Big Three. While
he urged Britain and the Soviet Union to accord such recognition
to the Chinese, neither Churchill nor Stalin shared the American
enthusiasm for China's potential. To make his point, Roosevelt,
while en route to the first Big Three meeting at Teheran, arranged
to confer with the Chinese leader, Chiang Kai-shek, at Cairo. (A
reluctant Churchill was also persuaded to attend.) And China, again
at American insistence, was given one of the five permanent seats
on the Security Council of the United Nations.

Although the United States treated China as a major power, the
Chinese had not yet earned such status. Chinese armies had been
unable to prevent Japanese conquest of most of northern and coastal
China, which included the major centers of population, industrial
areas, and ports. With large parts of China occupied by the Japanese,
the *Kuomintang* (or Nationalist) government, headed by Chiang
Kai-shek, retreated to mountainous southern China, where it established its wartime capital at Chungking. The Kuomintang exercised
nominal control over unoccupied China, but it was defied by local
military leaders, who exploited the peasantry, and challenged by
a communist movement headed by Mao Tse-tung, which steadily
increased its strength in rural areas. To Chiang, the communists
posed a danger far greater than the Japanese; the United States, he
assumed, would eventually defeat Japan. Hence, at a time when the
United States was directing its resources to the battle against Japan,
its principal Asian ally was preoccupied with preparing for the final
showdown in his long struggle against the communists.

American diplomatic and military personnel in wartime China
recognized the significance of these developments. They deplored

the massive corruption and inefficiency of the Kuomintang. That regime became increasingly repressive and appeared as brutal as the fascist nations against which the Allies were fighting. Conversely, the communist movement seemed to be progressive, introducing land reform in areas under its control. Moreover, the communist forces were fighting against the Japanese. Few astute observers doubted that the future of the country rested with the communists, not with the discredited Kuomintang.

These shortcomings of the Chinese war effort were virtually ignored in the United States, where the public continued to identify closely with the Chinese and with the government of Chiang Kai-shek in the struggle against the hated Japanese. Under the influence of wartime propaganda, Americans uncritically expected that China was progressing toward democracy and major-power status. When Americans were asked in 1942 which of twenty-five adjectives best described the Chinese, the predominant responses were "hardworking" (69 percent), "honest" (52 percent), and "brave" (48 percent).

Wartime news stories, motion pictures, and propaganda cultivated the image of the heroic Chinese resistance to the Japanese. A series of popular films, including *The Battle of China, Inside Fighting China, Ravaged Earth, Burma Convoy, A Yank on the Burma Road, China Girl,* and *God is My Co-pilot,* dramatized the common American and Chinese cause against the Japanese. When Madame Chiang Kai-shek visited the United States in 1943, she was enthusiastically received. After her emotional plea to Congress for more American support, "tough-guys melted," according to *Time,* and one congressman said, "God-damnit, I never saw anything like it. Madame Chiang had me on the verge of bursting into tears." In this atmosphere, the journalist Harold Isaacs notes, "a sympathetic image of the Chinese rose now to a unique pinnacle in a mass of American minds." The contrast between popular perception and reality could hardly have been sharper.

In fact, America's most pressing challenge was to get the Chinese to fight against the Japanese. Toward that end, Roosevelt sent General Joseph Stilwell to serve as chief of staff of the Kuomintang Army. Stilwell's plan to improve Chinese military prowess by reforming the army was resisted by Chiang and his generals. Stilwell and Chiang soon came to despise one another. To the American general, Chiang was a petty dictator (in the privacy of his diary, Stilwell contemptuously described him as "Peanut"). Stilwell's demands for reform threatened Chiang, who eventually demanded that Roosevelt recall Stilwell.

In addition to the Stilwell mission, the United States provided important air support for the Chinese, principally through the "over the hump" supply flights across the Himalayas from bases in India. Yet the Chinese always regarded American help as insufficient, and they were quick to contrast the low volume of supplies they were receiving with the great flow of American supplies to the Soviet Union and Great Britain.

Why didn't the United States provide the support that Chiang demanded? Might that have enabled him to fight more effectively against the Japanese? The failure to meet his demands resulted, in part, from the fact that the China theater had a low priority in the allocation of American resources. The Europe-first strategy dictated that the needs of European allies receive primary consideration. And in the greater Pacific theater, the needs of China ranked behind the navy's island campaign as well as MacArthur's New Guinea–Philippine campaign. Moreover, the United States considered its military assistance as its most effective leverage in forcing Chiang to fight more actively against the Japanese; increasing levels of support came to depend on evidence of Chinese willingness to fight the common enemy. The Kuomintang, however, always insisted that American support had to come first—only then could its armies fight effectively. "While the Americans refused to contribute more aid until the Chinese stepped up their war effort," the historian Warren Cohen writes, "the Chinese refused to step up their effort until they received more aid. At no time during the war was the circle broken."

American efforts to encourage political change led to similar frustrations. Whenever American officials warned Chiang of his declining popularity and urged reforms to counter communist appeal, the Chinese leader refused to accept responsibility for his domestic problems. Rather, he blamed the United States, charging that its policies were undermining his position. A special mission to China headed by Vice President Henry Wallace in the spring of 1944 failed to change Chiang's attitudes toward the problems facing his country.

The bankruptcy of the Kuomintang was underlined a few weeks later when the Japanese launched an offensive. The Chinese army was unwilling to fight, with large numbers fleeing or surrendering, enabling the Japanese to gain considerable territory, including the capture of several U.S. air bases. American patience ran out. It had become evident that the Kuomintang Army would never undertake any major offensive against the Japanese.

Still determined to see a strong China, Roosevelt, ever the realist, adjusted his means. Beginning in late 1944 he steered U.S. policy toward fostering a coalition government in which the communists would join with the Kuomintang. Given the deep-seated antagonism between those two groups, forming a coalition was an imposing task, and it eventually proved impossible. At the time, however, a coalition seemed the only solution to China's internal divisions. An important impetus for the coalition was the recommendations of American military and diplomatic personnel who had been impressed by the communist movement and had established a rapport with its leaders, Mao Tse-tung and Chou En-lai.

Besides cultivating a Kuomintang-communist coalition, Roosevelt also worked to make certain that the Soviet Union would become a partner in America's plans for postwar Asia. At the Yalta Conference, Roosevelt agreed to Stalin's demand for special concessions in China (particularly privileges in the province of Manchuria, an area of historic Russian interest). Such an allowance was considered necessary to help assure Soviet participation in the war against Japan. This concession, however, was an affront to Chinese sovereignty. "To dispose of Chinese territory without China's prior consent," Cohen observes, "was hardly calculated to make the Chinese rejoice." Yet Roosevelt also secured an important concession from Stalin that benefited Chiang's government: the Russian leader agreed to enter into a treaty of friendship and alliance with the Kuomintang. This was intended to enhance Chiang's status and to commit the Soviets to support a coalition government, as opposed to supporting only the communists. As he endeavored to salvage American expectations of China, Roosevelt recognized the difficulties confronting the United States in that endeavor. At Yalta he remarked to Stalin that, "for some time we have been trying to keep China alive." And by that time, the promotion of a coalition government and the involvement of the Soviet Union in that objective seemed the most feasible means of stabilizing China.

Ultimately, Roosevelt's visions of China failed to anticipate the rapidity of political change there that led, in less than five years after the end of World War II, to communist victory in the renewed civil war. And as Chiang was discredited, defeated, and forced from the Chinese mainland, the United States—as his benefactor—suffered an immense loss of prestige. The failure of Roosevelt's China policy, which only became fully evident after his death, reflected what the Department of State later wrote: "China was a problem for which there was no American solution."

The End of Colonialism

Roosevelt's final objective—promotion of the self-determination of colonial peoples—concerned the future of Asia and Africa. Western empires largely covered the area stretching from Southeast Asia to the Middle East and nearly the entire African continent. Parts of those empires had been disrupted by the war, in particular by the German-Italian encroachment in North Africa and the Japanese conquest of Southeast Asia.

The American government assumed that World War II would mark the end of Western imperialism. To Americans at home and those fighting overseas, the end of the Axis conquests had to bring as well an end to all forms of imperialism. A few months after the Pearl Harbor attack, Under Secretary of State Sumner Welles publicly expressed American sentiments:

> If the war is in fact a war for the liberation of peoples it must assure the sovereign equality of peoples throughout the world. . . .
> Our victory must bring in its train the liberation of all peoples. . . .
> The age of imperialism is ended. . . . The principles of the Atlantic Charter must be guaranteed to the world as a whole—in all oceans and in all continents.

This strong sense of anti-colonialism led the State Department, in its extensive planning for the postwar world, to anticipate that the imperial powers would be called upon to train their colonial peoples in self-government, leading eventually to independence. The American record in the Philippine Islands was advanced as the model for other imperial powers. After acquiring the Philippines, the United States had introduced substantial economic, social, and educational reforms. It also had provided for progressively greater self-government. Most important, the United States was committed to granting independence to the Philippines in 1946. Proud of its record there, the United States expected the British, French, Dutch, Portuguese, and Belgians to adopt similar policies toward their respective colonial possessions.

This immodest American plan implied a complete overhaul of the imperial system. Henceforth, imperial powers would have to accept "international accountability" for their actions; they would be expected, above all else, to prepare subject peoples in self-government and independence. Such expectations were resented by the European imperial powers who also happened to be America's wartime allies. The Europeans looked upon their empires as possessions; colonial policy was intended to benefit the home country's political and economic interests. Thus, American anti-colonialism triggered vigorous criticism, especially from the British, who held the largest empire and who, throughout the war, were in the best position to speak on behalf of the European imperial powers. The question of the future of the imperial system exemplified the "constant jealousies" that undermine wartime alliances.

Within the first few months after the Pearl Harbor attack, American sympathy with the cause of nationalism in India brought sharp differences with the British. India—the world's second most populous country and the heart of the British Empire— demanded independence. The nationalist movement, led by Mohandas Gandhi and Jawaharlal Nehru, enjoyed strong popular support and considerable international prestige. With Japan in control of neighboring Burma and threatening India, the Indians demanded independence immediately and rejected Britain's plan to defer it until after the war. To Churchill's consternation, Roosevelt sent a personal emissary to try to work out an agreement and pleaded with the prime minister to liberalize colonial policy. In the end, the British rejected American overtures and suppressed the Indian nationalist movement, jailing tens of thousands for the duration of the war.

The British silencing of India's call for independence was one of the dark pages of the Allied cause, for it cast doubt on the commitment to the freedom of subject peoples. Roosevelt, however, could not change Churchill's imperial mentality, which had formed nearly a half-century earlier when he had briefly been a colonial official in India. What a colleague described as "Winston's refusal to accept things as they are and not as they were in 1895" led to his disdain for India, its peoples, and leaders. He could not accept the proposition that Indians were capable of self-government, much less deserving of treatment as equals. To Churchill, Indians were "a beastly people with a beastly religion . . . the beastliest people in the world next to the Germans," and Gandhi was "a malignant subversive fanatic . . . a thoroughly evil force, hostile to us in every fiber . . . the world's most successful humbug." These sentiments led another official to write in his diary: "I am by no means quite sure whether on this subject of India Churchill is really quite sane."

Tragically, Churchill's disdain for India went beyond the suppression of the national movement and contributed to the loss of 3 million lives in a famine that in 1943 devastated rural Bengal in northeastern India (comprising the present-day nation of Bangladesh and the Indian state of West Bengal). In her book *Churchill's Secret War: The British Empire and the Ravaging of India During World War II* Madhusree Mukerjee, a science journalist, criticizes Churchill's imperviousness to the pleas from officials in India that the emergency in Bengal demanded the shipment of 80,000 tons of wheat a month. Churchill denied the request. Mukerjee points out while Churchill's government made food available for industrial and government workers in Calcutta, Bengal's major city, because those persons were considered vital to the war effort, it ignored the sufferings and starvation of the masses in the rural areas. "Despite the horrific ways in which they met their ends," she writes, "those Bengalis who perished in the villages did so in obscurity all but unnoticed by the national and international press." Put another way,

Mukerjee reiterates what other scholars of famines have contended: food supplies can always be found to prevent mass starvation. In Bengal in 1943, a British government, headed by the arch-imperialist Churchill, chose not to make that effort. The lofty ideals—the morality—of the Allies suffered accordingly.

While Churchill had his way in India, Roosevelt and other American officials focused on the future of imperialism in Southeast Asia. Japan's conquests of early 1942 gave it control of this vast region that included the colonies of Britain (Malaya, Burma); France (French Indochina, i.e., the present nations of Vietnam, Laos, Cambodia); the Netherlands (Netherlands East Indies, i.e., the present nation of Indonesia); and, of course, the United States (the Philippines). The British, French, and Dutch assumed that, at the end of the war, they would reestablish the old imperial order. The critical question was: Would it be a return to "business as usual" or would there be a commitment to self-government?

Among the countries of Southeast Asia, Roosevelt took a strong personal interest in the future of French Indochina. In fact, he wanted to assure that the French would not reestablish control over their former colony. By promoting international administration in the form of a "trusteeship," Roosevelt saw an opportunity to provide for training in self-government leading to eventual independence. Why did Roosevelt champion the cause of Indochina? First, he had little regard for the French, whom he believed had forfeited any claim to treatment as a major world power. France had been weak and ineffectual in the face of German aggression in 1940 and Japanese pressure on Indochina in 1940–41. Moreover, in Roosevelt's opinion the French were the worst of the imperial powers; he repeatedly said they shamelessly exploited the peoples of Indochina. Denial of French claims to Indochina was Roosevelt's way of punishing the French and of signaling their tarnished status on the world stage. Roosevelt's distaste for the French was intensified by his personal antagonism toward General Charles de Gaulle, the leader of the Free French. (This sentiment was not one-sided; de Gaulle also despised Roosevelt.)

Above all, Roosevelt meant to make certain that the principle of anti-colonialism would be achieved in at least one European-held colony. This was vital to Roosevelt after his failure to alter British policy in India. Now Roosevelt saw Indochina as an opportunity to prove that the war would truly mark the "end of imperialism." An international trusteeship for Indochina, together with the fulfillment of the American promise of Philippine independence, would thus serve as a stimulus for the advancement of colonial peoples generally.

To Roosevelt and other American officials, this commitment to anti-colonialism blended the idealism of the Allied cause with U.S. self-interest. Time was indeed running out on the capacity of the Western powers to govern distant peoples. The pledge of the Allies to self-determination of peoples and the weakening of all the European powers (regardless of the outcome of the war) was bound to give an irresistible momentum to nationalism in Asia and Africa. Roosevelt once expressed the essence of anti-colonialism when he told an adviser, "we can't afford to have one billion Asians hating us."

These American objectives for the colonial areas became the source of the most serious wartime tensions between the United States and Britain. On no other issue did the Americans and their closest ally find reconciliation of interest as intractable as in discussions of the future of Southeast Asia. "The differences between the two major Allies were indeed real and extensive enough," the British historian Christopher Thorne argues, "but they could at least have been clarified and faced more squarely. As it was, Southeast Asia remained an area where Anglo-American relations, so successful in many ways, were extremely poor."

As the war approached its end, the American government had to modify its plans for Southeast Asia. Since the region was not vital in the American plan to defeat Japan, the United States exercised little military influence there (except, of course, for the Philippines). Accordingly, responsibility for military operations in Southeast Asia was given to a British command. As happened in other areas of the world, military occupation soon led to political domination. The British reestablished their control in Burma and Malaya, assisted the French to retake Indochina, and helped the Dutch to regain the East Indies. As reality overcame idealism, the United States had to compromise with its Western European allies to assure postwar cooperation. In the end, the Americans agreed to a vague provision in the Charter of the United Nations that exhorted imperial powers to train subject peoples in self-government. Deferring to the British and other imperial powers, the United States rejected an alternative plan advanced by the Soviet Union that called for full national independence and self-determination in all colonial areas. Thus, by the end of the war the United States had retreated considerably from its earlier "end of imperialism" goal.

Yet in the long run Roosevelt's efforts against colonialism were prophetic. As the European imperial powers tried to resume "business as usual" in Southeast Asia, they found that the war had indeed brought fundamental changes heralding the end of imperialism. Japan's conquest discredited the Europeans and four years of Japanese administration had stimulated nationalist movements in various ways. Now the peoples of Southeast Asia demanded their independence and rejected the renewed pretensions of the European powers; in both Vietnam and Indonesia, nationalists proclaimed independence as the war ended, touching off wars against the French and Dutch that ended the days of imperialism. By that time, the United States had fulfilled its promise of independence to the Philippines and the British had liquidated their South Asian empire, leaving behind the independent nations of India, Pakistan, Ceylon (Sri Lanka), and Burma (Myanmar). This marked the beginning of the dramatic rise of new nations. Just two decades after the end of World War II, virtually all of Asia and Africa were free from European domination.

The United States, as the nation that championed self-determination throughout the greater part of the war, contributed to this irrepressible nationalism. While the European imperial powers may have gained some short-term advantages at the end of the war, it was the American vision for subject nations that was realized. For his role in championing self-determination, Roosevelt elevated American stature among peoples of Asia and Africa.

Franklin Delano Roosevelt died on April 12, 1945, just as the Allies stood on the threshold of victory. Throughout the last weeks of the war and into the immediate postwar era, Harry S. Truman, who succeeded to the presidency, endeavored to follow Roosevelt's policies. While Roosevelt's objectives were not fully achieved, his diplomatic leadership during the war represented the most effective expression of American interests that the circumstances permitted. The "practical idealist" did not accomplish all that he wished, but in large part he was successful. Politics is, after all, the art of the possible.

CHAPTER SIX

The Dilemmas of Victory

By early 1945 the Allies were winning the war. Germany and Japan were incapable of effective resistance but kept fighting until their leaders finally surrendered. Allied victories in Europe and Asia came in May and August respectively, bringing jubilation to the Allied peoples, who had endured much suffering and enormous losses of life.

Yet triumph also brought terribly sobering and troubling developments. With the victory in Europe, the Allies first learned the full extent of German persecution of European Jews. The discovery of the death camps and the realization that millions had been killed in a program of mass extermination led to outrage and intensified hatred of the Nazi regime. This shock eventually led to questions of whether the Allies could have used their powers to stop, or at least limit, the cruelties of the Holocaust. And in the final days of the war against Japan, when the United States dropped atomic bombs on two Japanese cities, questions arose about the necessity of this first, and thus far only, use of atomic weapons in warfare. In sum, the issues surrounding the death camps and the atomic bomb cast doubt on the morality of American warfare.

Victory in Europe and the
Extent of Nazi Tyranny

With Russian armies advancing from the east and the western Allies from the west, the German empire collapsed. Although still offering some futile resistance, German forces were outnumbered and poorly supplied. Their leader spent his last days in an underground shelter in Berlin. As the Russians surrounded the city, Hitler at last recognized the impending defeat, but characteristically refused to bear responsibility for surrendering to the Allies. In his final acts on April 30, he wrote a testimony reiterating his twisted beliefs, appointed Admiral Karl Doenitz as his successor, and then took his own life. By that time, Berlin was about to fall to the Russians, while American forces had reached the banks of the Elbe. On May 8 Germany surrendered. Hitler's "thousand-year Reich" had lasted twelve years.

In that brief span of time, Nazism had brought incredible death and destruction. The victory in Europe exposed the extent of Nazi atrocities. The Allied armies advancing into the Third Reich uncovered the death camps where millions of persons had been systematically killed. Jews were the principal victims of the warped ideology of Nazism, but the Holocaust also included the extermination of other "undesirables"—gypsies, homosexuals, the mentally and physically disabled, common criminals, and political opponents. Altogether 6 million Jews and an almost equal number of others perished in the death camps, some of which had the capacity to kill as many as 12,000 to 25,000 persons daily.

In the death camps, Allied troops found the bodies of recent victims of gas chambers, where men, women, and children of all ages had died, as well as the starving survivors. Even at a time when humankind had become insensitive to mass killing, the revelations of the Holocaust were numbing. In his massive work, *A World at Arms: A Global History of World War II*, the historian Gerhard L. Weinberg places this moment in perspective: "Here was something quite different from the specific massacres. . . . Here were the most tangible signs of a general horror in a form the ordinary person could only try to grasp."

General Dwight D. Eisenhower, the commander of Allied forces, realized the imperative that this monstrous evil be witnessed and recorded, so it would never be forgotten. He ordered that Allied soldiers and German civilians be brought to the death camps and that the piles of corpses and the emaciated survivors be filmed. He said: "We are told that the American soldier does not know what he is fighting for. Now, at least, he will know what he is fighting against." In a letter to Chief of Staff George C. Marshall, Eisenhower explained: "The things I saw beggar description. The visual evidence and the verbal testimony of starvation, cruelty and bestiality were overpowering. I made the visit deliberately in order to be in a position to give firsthand evidence of these things if ever, in the future, there develops a tendency to charge these allegations merely to 'propaganda.'"

The American soldiers who liberated many of the camps could barely comprehend the scenes they confronted. One American soldier wrote to his parents: "Our first sight was what looked like cordwood piled up along the side of a long wall. We quickly realized, to our horror, that is was naked dead people who were so thin they hardly looked human. The pile was five or six feet high and several hundred feet long. And then there were the survivors—they looked like walking skeletons."

As part of the first squad to enter the large Buchenwald camp, one soldier wrote of piles of corpses left behind by the Germans who had fled a few hours earlier: "It was like entering Hell. On one wagon alone, we counted almost 100 bodies. I guess the crematorium couldn't take them fast enough." Another GI talked about the survivors: "We kept saying to the emaciated prisoners, 'You're free, you're free.' And they looked so dumbfounded like, 'How can that be?'—like they were born in that hellhole." A comrade wrote to his family: "Every day for the rest of my life, what I've witnessed here will be the first thing I remember and the last thing I forget." Gruesome images of the dead and the survivors of the concentration camps—captured on newsreel films shown in movie theaters and in photographs in news magazines, particularly *Life*—were etched indelibly into the consciousness of Americans. For years, reports of the death camps had reached the outside world, but they had been largely discounted as exaggerated, and the extent of the extermination of European Jewry had never been understood. Reporting on the unfolding horror, *Time* magazine noted: "For 12 years the enemies of totalitarianism had told the world of these horrors. They were past belief. But the evidence of the camps at Buchenwald, Belsen, Erla, and Nordhausen was as irrefutable as death, as monstrous as human degradation."

As the full dimensions of the Holocaust became known, questions were eventually raised about whether the Allies, especially the United States, might have lessened the extent of this barbarism. What could the United States have done? First, prior to American involvement in the war, the United States could have liberalized its immigration policy to permit escape from Nazism. From the time that Hitler came to power in 1933, Nazis had persecuted Jews in Germany and later in other countries over which Germany gained control. While some groups in the United States tried to get special legislation through Congress that would have permitted the admission of refugees, labor groups and others, concerned over the scarcity of jobs during the Depression, lobbied against loosening immigration quotas on the grounds that it would hurt American workers.

Moreover, suggestions of assistance to Jews encountered a strong undercurrent of anti-Semitism in American cultural and political life. The Roosevelt administration, confronting a host of domestic and international problems in the 1930s, gave no priority to relaxing immigration policy. Hence, Jewish refugees seeking asylum in the United States confronted a consistently hostile situation. Tragically, hundreds of thousands of people who might have come to the United States in the 1930s lost their lives in the death camps.

With Germany's conquests of 1940–41 bringing millions of additional Jews under its control, the Nazis in 1942 began the Final Solution, a euphemism for systematic extermination of Europe's Jews. News from German-controlled areas was fragmentary at best, but Jewish leaders in the United States and high-ranking U.S. officials received reliable information of the forced deportation of Jews to concentration camps. As the Nazis carried out their extermination policy, Jews desperately sought to flee Europe and looked to the United States for transportation and asylum. Jewish leaders also urged the U.S. government to undertake a rescue effort and liberalize immigration policy to permit entry of refugees. The State Department resisted these pressures, and President Franklin D. Roosevelt, too, was reluctant to take any action. Under pressure from the Secretary of the Treasury Henry Morgenthau and congressional leaders who warned him that his administration faced a scandal over its indifference to the plight of the Jews, Roosevelt in 1944 established the War Refugee Board, which worked with Jewish organizations in the United States and overseas. Although the War Refugee Board did play a role in saving about 200,000 European Jews, its director later reflected, "What we did was little enough. . . . Late and little, I would say."

The limited U.S. assistance to the European Jews reflected in part an inability to comprehend the extent of the Nazi extermination program. It was assumed there would be only sporadic killings and that most of the Jews detained by the Nazis would be enslaved as war workers. But the failure to aid the Jews went deeper than American inability to fathom the depth of Nazi tyranny. Some U.S. officials feared an influx of destitute Jewish settlers and claimed inadequate facilities to bring Jews to America. That rationale was specious. Most transportation ships carried goods to Europe but returned empty. Moreover, there were no problems finding the ships to transport 400,000 prisoners of war and 100,000 non-Jewish refugees across the Atlantic.

Leaders of Jewish and other groups also pressed the British and Americans to bomb the rail lines leading to the death camps themselves and the gas chambers within the camps. Military officials, however, maintained that such attacks would divert resources and delay victory over Germany, which, they argued, was the only certain way to save the remaining Jews.

The military leadership took the position that "rescuing victims of enemy oppression [would not be allowed] unless such rescues are the direct result of military operations conducted with the objective of defeating the enemy's armed forces." That justification, however, is not persuasive. The fight against the Axis powers often took into consideration nonmilitary considerations, such as decisions not to bomb two cities in order to preserve artistic treasures and medieval architecture and to divert troops to save prized horses in Austria. A Zionist leader asked: "If horses were being slaughtered as are the Jews of Poland, there would by now be a loud demand for organized action against cruelty to animals. Somehow, when it concerns Jews everyone remains silent." Indifference blended with anti-Semitism in the American military leadership to dismiss any suggestion of using military power on behalf of the Holocaust victims. As historian David Wyman documents in *The Abandonment of the Jews*, the military leadership, despite its claims to the contrary, never undertook a study of the feasibility of bombing the death camps. In *The 'Jewish Threat': Anti-Semitic Politics of the U.S. Army*, historian Joseph Bendersky writes that the army "never pursued any systematic examination of the proposals presented to it, nor did it ask theater commanders what might have been done."

Perhaps most important, the plight of the Jews concerned only a few Americans. While a number of Jewish leaders were active, others failed to press the case. Christian church leaders, too, rarely raised their voices. In all, a profound indifference helped to doom Europe's Jews.

"The Greatest Thing in History": The Atomic Bomb and Japan's Surrender

On the morning of August 6, 1945, an American B-29 named the *Enola Gay* reached its target: the city of Hiroshima, Japan. Its single bomb, called "Little Boy," weighed 10,000 pounds and had a destructive capacity of 20,000 tons of TNT. Behind that mission to Hiroshima lay four years of atomic research and development— "the best kept secret of the war." The so-called Manhattan Project had culminated three weeks earlier, on July 16, in the secret and successful testing of an atomic device in the remote desert of New Mexico. On July 26 the United States, through the Potsdam Declaration, demanded that Japan surrender unconditionally or face "prompt and utter destruction." When the Japanese failed to surrender, President Truman ordered atomic warfare.

The *Enola Gay* dropped the bomb above the center of Hiroshima, a commercial and manufacturing city which, until that moment, had largely been spared destruction. Just as the 350,000 people of Hiroshima were going about their early morning tasks, the bomb exploded about 2,000 feet above the city. Suddenly, a blinding light flashed across the sky. Next came a burst of intense heat traveling at the speed of sound. The heat from the explosion instantly incinerated thousands of people, leaving only their charred remains. Thousands more died from subsequent burns and wounds and the effects of radioactive contamination.

After the wave of unbearable heat, a concussive blast slammed outward—with the force of a 500-mile-per-hour wind—leveling everything in its path. The heat and the blast ignited area-wide fires. In a few moments the sky rained strange, black cinders the size of marbles. Finally, the fierce "fire wind" blew intensely hot air (fueled further by the fires raging throughout the city) back toward the center of the explosion, destroying buildings, uprooting trees, and killing still more people. The river then heaved into enormous waves, drowning persons who had fled to the water. Overhead, a giant mushroom cloud grew to monstrous size, blackening the sky.

In minutes the city of Hiroshima had become smoking, radioactive rubble. Only one-fifth of its buildings survived the attack. But what the attack did to human beings was most significant and most gruesome. About 100,000 people were killed immediately by or died within hours of the explosion and an equal number were wounded. Those who survived were thrust into a waking nightmare. A Japanese doctor, himself badly wounded, recalled that "no one talked, and the ominous silence was relieved only by a subdued rustle among so many people, restless, in pain, anxious, and afraid, waiting for something else to happen." The survivors were badly burned, their skin peeling off, and they suffered from nausea, diarrhea, and intense thirst.

Upon learning of the Hiroshima attack, Truman described the atomic bomb as the "greatest thing in history." Certainly it was the most destructive weapon ever devised by humankind, and on that August morning in 1945 the world had hurtled into the atomic age. Three days later, on August 9, the U.S. Military dropped another atomic bomb on Japan. The people of Nagasaki, a port and steel-manufacturing city of 250,000 inhabitants, became the second group of victims of atomic warfare. Another 75,000 men, women, and children perished within hours of the attack and some 50,000 were wounded. The bomb used against Nagasaki was actually more powerful than the one dropped on Hiroshima, but because of local terrain, it caused less damage and fewer casualties than had the first. The point of atomic warfare, however, had been made: the United States seemed poised to level Japanese cities one at a time. Beyond staggering casualties caused immediately by the bombings of Hiroshima and Nagasaki, another 130,000 people in those two cities died from injuries and radioactive illness during the next five years.

Shortly after the bombings the Japanese at last indicated a willingness to surrender. The end of the war in the Pacific—popularly known as VJ Day—came on August 14.

In the immediate aftermath of the attacks on Hiroshima and Nagasaki, most Americans agreed with Truman that the atomic bomb was "the greatest thing in history." Public opinion polls in late 1945 reported 75 to 85 percent approval of the use of the bomb. Many Americans said that more atomic bombs should have been dropped. Such attitudes reflected the deep-felt hatred of the Japanese. In the minds of many, Hiroshima and Nagasaki seemed a just retribution for the Pearl Harbor attack and the Bataan Death March. As Truman said two days after the Nagasaki strike, "When you have to deal with a beast, you have to treat him as a beast." Moreover, popular support was reinforced by the assumption that by quickly ending the war and rendering unnecessary an invasion of Japan, the use of the bomb had spared thousands of American lives. Thus, in the emotionalism of the day, the bombings of Hiroshima and Nagasaki seemed both appropriate and necessary.

Only a year after VJ Day, however, the American conscience over Hiroshima and Nagasaki was pricked. The writings of war correspondent John Hersey, who visited Hiroshima and interviewed survivors, exposed the horrors of atomic warfare. First appearing in serialized fashion in *The New Yorker*, his best-selling *Hiroshima* had a profound effect on the attitudes of Americans. "For perhaps the first time since Pearl Harbor," historian Michael Yavenditti writes, "thousands of Americans confronted Japanese who were ordinary human beings and who manifested few of the stereotyped Japanese warrior traits of fanaticism and sadism." One university student wrote that prior to reading Hersey's account, "I had never thought of the people in bombed cities as individuals." What Hersey did was to give survivors the opportunity to describe their experience of August 6, 1945: the surprise of the bombing, the fire storm, the absence of medical services, and the terrible fear, blood, pain, and confusion. While it would be incorrect to state that Hersey's book changed public thinking, it forced conscientious Americans to reconsider their government's actions of August 6 and 9, 1945.

Hiroshima and Nagasaki: The Lingering Questions

The devastating effects of the Hiroshima and Nagasaki atomic bombings, so vividly told by Hersey (and later by others), came to trouble many Americans and eventually raised questions about the use of those first atomic weapons. Admiral William D. Leahy, a presidential adviser, expressed the doubts of many when he wrote: "In being the first to use it, we had adopted the ethical standard common to the barbarians of the Dark Ages. I was not taught to make war in that fashion, and wars cannot be won by destroying women and children."

The long debate over Hiroshima and Nagasaki has centered on several questions: Were the bombs necessary to end the war? Might this new weapon have been used less destructively? Were the bombings immoral? Did the United States engage in atomic warfare for reasons other than to force Japan's surrender? How did the American government reach its decision to use the bombs? Even if use of the first atomic bomb had been justified, was dropping the second bomb, in any sense, necessary?

On the first issue—*were the bombs necessary to end the war?*— American officials disagreed considerably over Japan's capacity to continue the war. Many believed that only an invasion of the home islands would convince Japan to surrender. They fully expected repetition of the desperate resistance shown during the island fighting, including the kamikaze tactic. Recent battles on Iwo Jima and Okinawa appeared to foreshadow the kind of defense the Japanese would make on their home islands; therefore, a home-island invasion surely would have taken a large toll of both American and Japanese lives. Assuming that the only alternative to an invasion was the use of the atomic bombs, American and Japanese casualties from the invasion would have far exceeded the losses at Hiroshima and Nagasaki.

The Truman administration quickly made this claim its rationale for the atomic bombings. Partly to counter the impact of Hersey's book, former secretary of war Henry Stimson wrote an influential article in 1947 contending that the atomic bombings had been necessary to preclude an invasion of Japan that likely would have produced 1 million American casualties. And Truman himself always justified his decision on those grounds, in his words: "It was a question of saving hundreds of thousands of American lives." That explanation, however, oversimplifies the situation facing the United States in the summer of 1945. A number of officials questioned the need for an invasion. The American blockade and air attacks, they argued, had reduced Japan to the point where it could not continue the war much longer. With its industry in shambles, its raw materials and food supplies shut off, and its navy and air force decimated, Japan was so weak that continuing the war was not only hopeless but impossible. Shortly after the war ended, an American military survey of Japan concluded "certainly prior to 31 December 1945, and in all probability prior to 1 November 1945, Japan would have surrendered even if the atomic bombs had not been dropped . . . and even if no invasion had been planned or contemplated."

Often ignored in the calculation of lives "lost" or "saved" by the atomic bombings is that the Japanese and Americans were not the only peoples fighting. Japan was still conducting its military operations in China and parts of Southeast Asia, campaigns responsible for untold numbers of casualties, most of them civilian. The longer the war continued, the greater the casualties in those areas. Richard B. Frank, the author of *Downfall: The End of the Imperial Japanese Empire*, underscores the carnage beyond Japan:

> In China alone . . . there was an average of 3,000 to 4,500 deaths per day, or between 100,000–150,000 per month. Enormous numbers of other Asians were likewise dying. Then we come to Allied

civilian internees and POWs at risk from abuse and starvation. In any debate over the morality or immorality of the use of atomic weapons . . . it is critical that all the noncombatant deaths be considered. If it is proper to weigh the costs in noncombatant lives in two cities in the aggressor nation, it is at least proper to consider the noncombatants in victim nations.

While the casualties increased daily, the Japanese were moving, albeit hesitantly and indirectly, toward surrender. Recognizing their country's position, a political faction determined to end the war gained influence within the Japanese government. In April 1945, a new cabinet under Admiral Baron Suzuki, the eighty-year-old leader of the peace faction, came to power: Reportedly, Emperor Hirohito also favored an end to the war. Through contacts with the Soviet Union, which was still ostensibly neutral, Japan tried to initiate negotiations with the United States. Stalin, however, brushed aside the overtures. Committed to entering the war against Japan, which promised the Soviet Union political gains in Asia, he had no interest in helping the beleaguered Japanese end the war. Moreover, the Japanese leadership remained divided and obstinate, dooming any prospects for negotiation. The ultranationalists resisted surrender and urged continued fighting. Even those most interested in stopping the war rejected the American demand of "unconditional surrender" and insisted that the emperor should be permitted to retain his traditional position.

Since the invasion was not scheduled until November 1, the United States had time to pursue Japan's surrender through diplomatic means. Further, when the war did end, the United States ironically accepted "conditional surrender" by permitting the emperor to continue in his position. On the use of atomic weapons, military historian Hanson Baldwin argues:

> The "decision" . . . was a pretty hasty one. . . . We were twice guilty. We dropped the bomb at a time when Japan was already negotiating for an end to the war but before those negotiations could come to fruition. We demanded unconditional surrender, then dropped the bomb and accepted conditional surrender, a sequence which indicates pretty clearly that the Japanese would have surrendered

even if the bomb had not been dropped, had the Potsdam Declaration included our promise to permit the Emperor to remain on his imperial throne.

Assuming that the United States wanted to take advantage of its new weapon to force an early surrender, *were there means available other than the bombing of urban centers*? Rather than killing and injuring thousands of persons, the United States might merely have demonstrated the destructive capacity of its new weapon. This alternative was advanced by a group of atomic scientists who had been involved in the Manhattan Project. As the project neared completion, these scientists grew concerned about the postwar implications of atomic warfare and the potential for a nuclear arms race. Determined that the United States should not establish the precedent for using atomic weapons, they urged that the U.S. Military should demonstrate the atomic bomb by detonating one on a remote island or barren desert with invited Japanese and other international representatives on hand to observe it.

Practical objections undermined this alternative. First, what if the demonstration bomb did not detonate? The possibility of failure was a persistent fear. Such an incident would only encourage Japanese resistance and invite criticism from the other Allies. Second, would the demonstration bomb, even if successfully detonated, have compelled a Japanese surrender? Many American officials, led by Secretary of War Stimson, firmly believed that only a direct attack could force capitulation. After all, they argued, the Japanese had kept fighting despite the massive air bombings of their cities; why should a distant demonstration bomb cause immediate surrender? Third, would a demonstration bomb be a needless "waste"? The United States had only three atomic bombs: one built for the July 16 test, and the two built for use in early August. No others were to be built until later that month. "Wasting" a bomb with a demonstration would leave only one for military use should the Japanese refuse to surrender. Hence, officials rejected the demonstration alternative.

Implicit in the questions of "necessity" and "alternatives" is a moral consideration: *Were the atomic bombings an immoral act?* As soon as the evidence of mass destruction, death, and radioactive contamination became known, many Americans were aroused by the moral implications of their government's action. Writing in 1945, Dwight Macdonald discounted any moral justification:

> Such moral defenses are offered as: the war was shortened and many lives saved; . . . the Japanese deserved it because they started the war; . . . they refused to surrender. The flimsiness of these justifications is apparent; any atrocious action, absolutely any one, could be excused on such grounds. For there is really only one possible answer to the problem posed by Dostoievski's Grand Inquisitor: if all mankind realize eternal and complete happiness by torturing to death a single child, would this act be justified?

From that perspective, the bombings lacked any moral substance. In an absolute sense, the act was immoral, but, in the midst of total war, how does one draw the line between "moral" and "immoral" actions? By 1945, the killing of civilians had become an accepted part of Allied bombing strategy. The fire bombings of Japanese cities, beginning with the massive March 9–10 attack on Tokyo, had already taken a staggering toll of civilian casualties.

Furthermore, wanton destructiveness was not restricted to the war against Japan. Prior to Germany's surrender, its cities had been leveled. For instance, a massive Allied bombing of Dresden in February of 1945 destroyed nearly the entire city. In bombings like those of Tokyo and Dresden, the actual military gains were nominal; rather, the intent was to demonstrate Allied power and demoralize civilian populations. Hence, the difference between the bombings of Hiroshima and Nagasaki, on one side, and the lethal bombings of other cities, on the other, was not in total casualties but in the means: a single bomb of virtually unlimited destructive capacity and producing radioactive fallout, rather than hundreds of bombs, each of which had limited destructive potential. By the end of a conflict in which so many innocent lives had been lost, American officials had become desensitized to moral considerations. They no longer seemed relevant.

In supporting the argument that the atomic bomb was used unnecessarily and hastily, a few scholars have posed another troubling question: *Did the United States engage in atomic warfare for reasons other than forcing the surrender of Japan?* Maintaining that the use of the bomb must be viewed within the context of international relations, some argue that the United States saw its new weapon as a means of countering the power of the Soviet Union. After the end of the war in Europe, differences between the Soviet Union and the United States over a number of issues began to undermine wartime unity. Gar Alperovitz, in the influential book *Atomic Diplomacy*, contends that political, rather than military, considerations explain the use of the atomic bombs. "Atomic diplomacy" had two objectives. First, by using the bombs quickly, the United States precluded the necessity of Soviet participation in the war against Japan. The Russians were obliged to enter the war in Asia within three months after the defeat of Germany, or by August 8 (which indeed was the date of the Russian declaration of war against Japan), but by hastening Japan's surrender, the United States was making certain that Russia's help would not be needed and, as a result, that its influence in Asia would remain limited. Second, the A-bomb promised diplomatic benefits in Europe as well. This awesome display of American power, it has been argued, offered a means—albeit an unsuccessful one in hindsight—of coercing the Russians into acceptance of American demands for democratic governments in Eastern Europe. Put simply, "atomic diplomacy" was a means of intimidating the Soviets.

This interpretation suggests that the United States killed some 200,000 Japanese, at least in part, to prove its prowess to the Soviet Union. The "atomic diplomacy" argument, which has been highly controversial, generally fails to stand the test of rigid analysis. Evidence from government files confirms that the use of the bomb was considered necessary, and that there was no acknowledged anti-Soviet motive determining American action. As one critic has written, atomic diplomacy amounts to "believing the unbelievable."

Nonetheless, questioning whether concern about the Soviet Union was the principal reason for the use of the atomic bomb does not preclude the possibility that American officials saw it as a secondary reason. From the beginning of the Manhattan Project, the United States, while planning a postwar atomic monopoly with Great Britain, chose not to inform the Soviet Union of its atomic program. Hence, a practice had developed of considering atomic policy as a means of keeping the Russians in line. Within that context, Martin Sherwin argues in *A World Destroyed: The Atomic Bomb and the Grand Alliance*:

> [American officials] consciously considered two diplomatic effects of a combat demonstration of the bomb: first, the impact of the attack on Japan's leaders, who might be persuaded thereby to end the war; and, second, the impact of that attack on the Soviet Union's leaders who might then prove to be more cooperative. It is likely that the contemplation together of the anticipated effects upon both Japanese and Soviet leaders was what turned aside any inclination to question the use of the bomb. Perhaps then the demonstration of American power to the Soviet Union offered an additional benefit—a "diplomatic bonus"—to be derived from the strategic use of the atomic bomb.

These issues lead to the question: *How did the American government decide to use the atomic bomb?* This momentous decision was made without any major debate among policy makers over those implications of atomic warfare that have since become important. The prevailing assumption among those who were aware of the Manhattan Project was that whenever the bomb was developed and tested, it would be used. Rarely was that assumption questioned. Truman, the man responsible for the decision, learned that the project was nearing completion after becoming president on April 12, 1945, but he made no effort either to understand the implications of atomic warfare or to control the decision-making process. General Leslie Groves, director of the project who had a vested interest in justifying the years of research and enormous costs, never brought alternatives to Truman's attention. Given the momentum of the project, Truman's authority, in practice, was limited to halting the use of the bomb. But he had no inclination to do so. When Secretary Stimson and General Groves brought the president a lengthy report on the bomb's progress in May of 1945, Truman said: "I don't like to read long reports. Your present course is sound. Carry on as you are doing now." Behind that statement was Truman's unquestioned assumption, which he set forth in his memoirs: "Let there be no mistake about it. I regarded the bomb as a military weapon and never had any doubt that it should be used."

The same attitude prevailed among the members of a small group, known as the Interim Committee, which was appointed to advise Truman on atomic policy. The Interim Committee focused on the question of how, rather than whether, to use the bomb; use of atomic weapons was a foregone conclusion. In that atmosphere the report of a group of scientists recommending a demonstration bomb prior to combat use received only brief attention. Likewise, the situation discouraged full discussion of the "necessity" and "moral" issues involved. With the "greatest thing in history" at their disposal, American officials never questioned whether they should employ it. The decision to use the atomic bomb was, in essence, a "decision by indecision."

The bombing of Hiroshima and Nagasaki, then, is best explained by the circumstances in which it was developed. Stimson later recalled: "At no time, from 1941 to 1945, did I ever hear it suggested by the President, or by any other responsible member of the government, that atomic energy should not be used in the war." In his history of the war, Winston Churchill wrote: "The historic fact remains . . . that the decision whether or not to use the atomic bomb to compel the surrender of Japan was never even an issue." Atomic scientist J. Robert Oppenheimer stated succinctly: "The decision was inherent in the project."

Finally, one more troubling question remains: *Even if the first atomic bomb can be justified, was the second bombing, in any sense, necessary?* The stated reason for the bombing of Nagasaki, just three days after Hiroshima had been destroyed, was to force an immediate surrender. Indeed, the American government considered the use of both of its atomic bombs as part of the same operation. After Hiroshima, Truman warned the Japanese to "expect a rain of ruin from the air, the like of which has never been seen on this earth." And the attack on Nagasaki seemingly demonstrated the American capacity to destroy one Japanese city after another. But the Japanese government was already on the cusp of surrender prior to the Nagasaki attack; the peace faction had steadily increased its influence. The Hiroshima attack, followed two days later by the Russian declaration of war against Japan, had left even the most militant Japanese no choice but to call an end to the war. The shock of the events of August 6 and 8 disrupted the normal functioning of the Japanese government, but the imperative to surrender was widely recognized and the situation lent itself to a rare display of leadership on the part of the emperor, whose influence forced the surrender decision. So for its haste in dropping a second atomic bomb, the Truman administration faces perhaps the strongest criticism of its atomic warfare. "[N]either bomb may have been necessary," Sherwin observes, "and certainly the second one was not." The historian Richard B. Rhodes disagrees, arguing that it was only after the Nagasaki attack that the emperor was able to insist on the imperative of surrender, which military leaders had resisted even in the face of the Hiroshima bombing and the Soviet Union's entry.

A People Victorious: America at the End of the War

When the war ended in 1945, however, questions about whether the United States might have done more to help European Jews or have avoided the use of atomic weapons were not vital issues. The terrible war—a conflict that had taken 325,000 American lives—was, at long last, over. The American people, aggrieved and relieved at the same time, were justifiably proud of a considerable accomplishment and looked to the future with optimism. The mood of America as it entered the postwar era was represented in the very popular, Academy Award–winning motion picture *The Best Years of Our Lives*, which focused on the experiences of three returning servicemen and their families. While the film treated the problems of adjustment to civilian life realistically, it ended on an optimistic tone. And in some ways that generation of Americans *was* entering its "best years," for the postwar period witnessed substantial development of the national economy and, by the 1950s, a higher standard of living for millions of middle-class Americans. As people moved to the suburbs and increased their level of consumer spending, the majority of Americans had become part of what would be described as the "affluent society."

Yet in other ways the postwar by no means constituted the "best years." Internationally, the United States and Russia became antagonists in a Cold War that was to last for more than forty years and lead to an enormously costly and frightening nuclear arms race. As Americans watched with apprehension the Soviets establish firm control over much of Central and Eastern Europe, many wondered what had gone so wrong. Even more disquieting was the communist victory in the renewed Chinese civil war, which led to the establishment of the People's Republic in 1949 and the ouster of Chiang Kai-shek and his nationalists to the small island of Taiwan. A year later the United States found itself again at war in a confusing, limited conflict in Korea. At home the postwar period brought much labor unrest, corruption in government, and one of the ugliest episodes of American history—a "Red Scare" touched off by reckless charges of widespread communist influence in government and the entertainment industry. The resultant anticommunist witch hunt divided Americans, undermined civil liberties, and destroyed the careers of many loyal Americans.

In some ways, perhaps Americans' "best years" had been the war years themselves. Despite the deaths and casualties on battlefields around the world, for four years all Americans stood united in a common cause. Among the men and women at home and overseas, the war gave direction and meaning to lives as nothing else has before or since. The war years were, to borrow a line from Charles Dickens, "the best of times and the worst of times." Everyone wanted the fighting to end victoriously, and the surrender of the Axis meant that an evil enemy had been utterly destroyed. Yet the issues that had been so clear from the day of the Pearl Harbor attack were now part of the past. Never again would life be so simple.

CONCLUSION

Why the Allies Won

It is difficult to comprehend the extent of the death and destruction caused by the war. The total number of people killed has been estimated at 60 million. Throughout the conflict more civilians than combatants lost their lives, including the Holocaust's 6 million Jewish victims (about one-third of the world's Jewish population) and an equal number of "undesirables." Millions of other people were caught in the crossfire between armies, buried under the rubble caused by air raids, or wantonly slaughtered by invading forces. The Soviet Union suffered, by far, the heaviest losses; they are now estimated at 25 million deaths, two-thirds of whom were civilians. Germany's total losses approximated 4 million. The heavy Soviet and German casualties are testimony to the intensity of the Eastern Front warfare. Of Germany's 2.8 million military deaths, 2.4 million of them were incurred in the fighting against the Soviet Union. So in the four years of the Eastern Front fighting, the combined German and Soviet military losses alone approached 11 million. Peoples caught between the Soviets and Germans also suffered enormously; the Polish, the most vulnerable, lost 6 million people, nearly half of whom were victims of the Holocaust. Yugoslavia's deaths approached 2 million. Rumania, Hungary, and Czechoslovakia each lost hundreds of thousands, including substantial numbers of their men who had been forced to fight for the Axis. Italy's deaths totaled 400,000.

The fighting in Asia also took an enormous toll on human life. Japan lost 2 million people. China's casualties, the most difficult to calculate, have been estimated as low as 2.5 million and as high as 15 million, with the higher figure now regarded as the more accurate. In addition, the peoples of Southeast Asia suffered substantial losses during the Japanese conquest and rule.

Other Allied losses pale in comparison with those of the Soviet Union and China. British deaths reached about 400,000. (Other Commonwealth deaths—including military units from Canada, Australia, New Zealand, and India—totaled 200,000). The French, including their forces in North Africa, lost about 580,000. American deaths, which included relatively few civilians, reached 325,000.

Beyond the deaths, the war left millions of people injured, including large numbers disabled for the remainder of their lives. The survivors included millions of refugees. Warfare had devastated cities, towns, roads, bridges, railways, and factories. The heaviest destruction was in Germany, the Soviet Union, and parts of Eastern Europe, China, and Japan. In short, the societies and economies of much of Europe and Asia lay in ruins.

The victorious Allies considered the enormous costs of war as the price necessary to purge the world of Adolph Hitler and his Nazism and the ultramilitant Japanese. Had Germany and Japan won the war and been able to impose their terms for peace on the United States, Great Britain, China, the Soviet Union, and the other Allies, much of the world would have been in the control of rigidly authoritarian rulers with no respect for the liberal values of Western civilization. Likely, the surviving nations would have been reduced economically and governed at the point of the Axis gun. The Allied peoples and their leaders—Franklin Roosevelt, Winston Churchill, and Josef Stalin—utterly rejected that alternative and therefore waged war to force the "unconditional surrender" of the Axis powers.

That objective was not easily achieved, but a remarkable transformation in the relative military strength of the Axis and Allies occurred between the beginning and the end of the war. From the spring of 1940 until late 1942, German and Japanese forces seemed unbeatable, as they systematically conquered the greater part of Europe and Asia respectively. Italy and lesser members of the Axis

added to the alliance's overall strength. Among other major powers, France was eliminated as a belligerent and China virtually so;
the Soviet Union, Great Britain, and the United States were ill-
prepared for war and early on their forces retreated before German and Japanese advances. Remarkably, within a relatively brief
period the military balance was completely reversed. The Germans
and Japanese were battered and retreating on all fronts, while the
Allies had completed a dramatic resurgence, dominating the fighting on land, sea, and air.

The military campaigns of the war tell the essential story of
where, when, and how the Allies overcame their disadvantages and
turned the tide in their favor. The outcome of those battles was
determined, to a large extent, by the influence of economic, strategic, political, and psychological factors. To understand the "why"
of the Allied victory requires looking behind the lines of battle at
the ways in which the major powers marshaled their physical and
human resources to wage all-out war. Four developments go far
toward explaining the Allied ascendancy.

(1) Industrial Supremacy: Achieving the Economic Potential

World War II was a "total war" in which the armies of belligerents and their entire societies and economies were fully mobilized.
Modern warfare requires a strong industrial base. From the beginning of the war, the Allies had a substantial overall potential advantage. A 1937 study of the relative war potential of leading industrial
countries calculated the following percentages of strength:

Country	Percent
United States	42%
Germany	14%
Soviet Union	14%
United Kingdom	10%
France	4%
Japan	4%
Italy	3%
Others	9%

In other words, a fully mobilized United States represented 42 percent of all the war-making potential in the world, three times that of Germany and fourteen times that of Japan. Adding the potential strength of the Soviet Union and the United Kingdom to that of the United States, the three principal Allies possessed 66 percent of the world's war-making potential: on the other side, Germany, Italy, and Japan represented only 21 percent. A key to the Allied advantage was its control of the world's supply of oil, a commodity described by an American geographer in 1943 as the "blood of battles that bring victory." The Axis held just 3 percent of the world's output of petroleum, while the Allies controlled 90 percent. This need for oil drove Axis offensives, notably in Japan's takeover of the Netherlands East Indies and Germany's drive to conquer the Caucasus region in the Soviet Union.

The enormous potential of the Allies was evident even in the early days in which they suffered defeats. To compensate for their relative industrial weakness, Germany, Italy, and Japan had concentrated far higher percentages of their national income on military spending in the late 1930s than had the British and Americans (the Soviets, both before and after the German attack in 1941, spent substantially on defense). Yet even in 1940, when the United States was just beginning to prepare for war and Great Britain was standing alone against the Germans, American and British aircraft production was almost double that of Germany, Japan, and Italy combined. In 1941–42, with the Soviet Union part of the Allied coalition, the Allies were out-producing the Axis in aircraft, major vessels, tanks, and armaments by wide margins—despite the Axis military advantage.

What the Allies, especially the United States and the Soviet Union, accomplished between 1942 and 1945 was to build on this economic advantage to realize their full war-making potential. In June 1941, Roosevelt told Congress, "With our national resources, our productive capacity, and the genius of our people for mass production, we will . . . outstrip the Axis powers in munitions of war." As he envisioned, the remarkable collaboration of government and the private sector transformed the economy and made the United States a military superpower. American industrial production, already the world's largest, doubled in size. The United States alone out produced the Axis states combined and provided the vast majority of Allied aircraft, tanks, trucks, artillery pieces, and naval vessels. The disparity was most striking in naval warfare, where the United States produced 6,775 vessels between 1942 and 1944, while Germany and Japan combined produced only 1,400.

The government of the Soviet Union achieved an equally impressive transformation of its economy. The Soviet accomplishment was all the more remarkable because the German invasion of 1941 had conquered the principal industrial, agricultural, and resource-bearing regions of the country. At this point the Soviet economy, which had ranked third in the world behind the United States and Germany, seemed on the verge of total collapse. The Soviet government, however, undertook a massive movement of some 1,500 plants, including their machinery, workers, and managers, eastward, away from the battles, where hastily improvised industrial centers were established. Despite the continuing German advance throughout 1942, the Soviets that year produced more weapons than their enemy. By 1943, they were out-producing Germany by a substantial margin.

The Allied superiority is underlined by comparative data of the production of various weapons from 1942 to 1945:

	Allies	Axis
Aircraft	506,000	157,000
Major Vessels	9,000	1,200
Tanks	195,000	55,500
Artillery	389,000	80,000

Contributing to the Allied industrial predominance was the underperformance of the Axis economies, particularly the German. This was ironic in that during the 1930s the Nazis had, more so than the government of any other nation, prepared their economy for warfare. The expansion of Nazi Germany in Central and Eastern Europe added to its raw materials and industrial base. With its own workforce mobilized, the Germans were poised to realize substantial industrial growth. But that did not happen. Suffering from complex governmental regulation and the incessant demands and interference of Nazi party officials and military leaders, the German economy stagnated, and production leveled off. Hitler tried to remedy the situation in 1943, but his reforms had only limited effect. By then Allied bombing was disrupting industrial production and causing social dislocations that further reduced the quality of the workforce's output.

Industrial supremacy, however, was not sufficient itself to assure Allied victory. Industrial powers have often failed to defeat enemies with weaker economic bases, as the United States later learned in Vietnam and the Soviet Union in Afghanistan. Yet relative economic strength is a vital factor in warfare, particularly when nations are engaged in "total war."

(2) Technology and Modernization of Armed Forces: Beating the Axis at Their Own Game

At the beginning of the war, the Axis, especially Germany, used armor and aircraft in ways that altered the concepts of warfare. Mechanization and technical improvements enabled the Germans to combine air power and ground force mobility with such efficiency that their *blitzkrieg* ("lightening strike") attack overran the Low Countries and France within a few weeks. The rapid Japanese sweep across Southeast Asia similarly overwhelmed ill-prepared Western defenders.

To reverse the military situation, the Allies had to imitate Axis techniques. The Soviet Union, the United States, and Great Britain built increasingly effective mechanized armies, developed improved bombers and fighters, and learned to better coordinate ground and air warfare.

When the initial German invasion almost completely destroyed its antiquated mechanized corps and air force, the Soviet Union started from scratch in rebuilding its armed forces. Premier Josef Stalin recognized the reasons for the German success; he told his countrymen in late 1941, "In modern warfare it is very difficult for the infantry to fight without tanks and without adequate protection from the air." The next year the Soviets concentrated their resources on the production of tanks and planes and their military leaders changed the ways they were employed. They built a new generation of tanks, developed improved bombers and fighters, and began coordination of air power with ground operations. Reinforcing the modernization of the Soviet Army was Lend-Lease assistance from the United States, which delivered more than half a million jeeps and trucks that provided the backbone of a motorized supply system. Lend-Lease also supplied telephone cable, radio stations, and field telephones that revolutionized military communications.

Paralleling the transformation of the Soviet military, the United States, within two years of the Pearl Harbor attack, built the most modern army and air force in the world. The commitment to a mechanized and motorized army built on the strength of the American automobile industry, which was by far the largest in the world and which in 1942 shifted completely to wartime production. Besides the production of army trucks and jeeps that provided the backbone of support for Allied forces, American industry also produced, as noted, prodigious numbers of tanks, naval vessels, and aircraft. Learning from their observations of Germany's early success, American military leaders, with Roosevelt's strong support, revolutionized the air force, developing a new generation of bombers, fighters, and fighter-bombers. And after some initial frustrations, the Americans also developed effective coordination of air and ground combat. The United States also took advantage of its access to oil to expand the production of high-octane fuel that enhanced the range and maneuverability of aircraft. By 1944, Americans produced 90 percent of the Allies' high-octane fuel, enabling them all to modernize their forces. During his meeting with Churchill and Roosevelt at Teheran, Stalin acknowledged the American role in modernizing the Allied forces, proposing a toast at one of the dinners: "This is a war of engines and octanes. I drink to the American auto industry and the American oil industry."

In one important way, the Allies carried reform of their armed forces beyond the Axis example. They devoted greater attention and resources to the noncombat operational areas of war: procurement, logistics, supplies, and military services. General George C. Marshall, the army chief of staff, divided the army into three separate components, each with equal status: ground forces, air forces, and services. The Soviets also gave attention to the service sector, whose head was on equal terms with combat commanders. The Allied attention to essential support of combat forces meant that their armies benefited from having better supplies, transportation, communications, medical treatment, and other services than did their enemies. In the Pacific theater, there were eighteen American noncombatant servicemen/women for every one man at the front; for the Japanese, the ratio was one to one. In Europe, the Americans had two service personnel for every one fighter; for the Germans, it was the reverse: two combatants for every one noncombatant. The disparities reflected in part the greater distances involved in moving American forces to fight in distant areas (notably more of a problem in the Pacific). But more important, they demonstrated the commitment to rapid support, supply, and replacement of soldiers. One German commander reported to his superiors during the Normandy invasion:

> I cannot understand these Americans. Each night we know that we have cut them to pieces, inflicted heavy casualties, mowed down their transport. But—in the morning we are suddenly faced with fresh battalions, with complete replacements of men, machines, food, tools, and weapons. This happens day after day.

Without the priority given to support, it would have been impossible for Allied forces to apply such sustained battlefield pressure.

The strength and the resourcefulness of American warfare reflected the spectacular growth of the armed forces. During the war, more than 16 million Americans (out of a total population of 140 million) wore uniforms, about 11 million as members of the army (which included the air force), 4 million in the navy, 670,000 as marines, and 360,000 in newly established women's military units.

Those units were part of the wartime transformation of the status of women as millions moved into the civilian work force, while thousands of others volunteered for military service. The first women's military units in American history—the WACS being the largest and best known—played an important auxiliary and support role for the combat forces. Women had served since 1901 in the Nurse Corps of the Army Medical Corps; the ranks of the Nurse Corps increased from 7,000 in 1941 to 57,000 by 1945. The exigencies of a global war led to broadening the role of women. Spurred partly by the example of the role of women in the British armed forces, U.S. military leaders established the Women's Army Corps (WACS), Women for Voluntary Emergency Service (WAVES), and Women Air Force Service Pilots (WASPS); although the marines and coast guard did not have women's units, they did include a few hundred women in their ranks. Women were excluded from combat, but many served overseas. General Douglas MacArthur praised the women's units as "our best soldiers," and General Dwight Eisenhower said that "their contributions in efficiency, skill, spirit, and determination are immeasurable."

The Allied military superiority resulted in part from the weaknesses of the Axis. Neither the Germans nor the Japanese were as strong as they appeared to be in the early fighting. When the Germans attacked the Soviet Union, their armored divisions were understrength and partly composed of obsolete tanks. Their support vehicles also were ill-suited for the terrain and weather. Hitler and his generals assumed that their soldiers had sufficient strength to achieve another easy victory, but once the Eastern Front became an extended campaign, the Germans were forced to rely increasingly on horses. German efforts to counter the effective tanks of the resurgent Soviet forces by developing newer models failed for various reasons, including the premature rushing of untested models into combat. Likewise, the German air force, suffering from inept leadership, invested heavily in newly developed models of bombers and fighters intended to match the improved Soviet aircraft, but these German prototypes turned out to be flops. Translated to the battlefield, the failures of the Germans to match Allied modernization meant that by 1944, German soldiers on the front line could no longer expect armored or air support.

Neither Italy nor Japan had the capability to keep pace with the rapid modernization of the major industrial powers. Both relied largely on horses. Their tank, aircraft, and other mechanized production was limited. Most of the Japanese army's trucks were imported American models, for which spare parts were no longer available. The Japanese weaponry also was obsolete, the main rifle dated to 1905, the heavy machine gun to 1914, and the light machine gun to 1922. These were no match against an American artillery barrage. The Japanese had insufficient resources to overcome their armed forces' lack of modernization. Japanese leaders' expectations that soldiers with superior fighting qualities could compensate for superior Allied weaponry were illusory.

The only hope for the Axis to redress their widening industrial and military imbalance was to develop a super weapon. By the late 1930s, it was widely recognized that atomic energy might produce a weapon of unprecedented destructive power. The Japanese undertook some preliminary research and experimentation, but they abandoned the project as too costly and unlikely to produce results within the likely timespan of the war. Germany, which prior to hostilities had been a center of atomic physics research, was more likely to undertake such a major commitment. Even as his scientists engaged in atomic-weapons research, Hitler was skeptical of the concept (partly because he saw physics as a "Jewish pseudoscience") and never gave the project a high priority. By war's end, Germany was years away from producing a working atomic weapon. On the other side, Roosevelt from early in the war gave unequivocal support to the development of the atomic bomb.

As in so many other aspects of the war, the Allies benefited from the mistakes of the Axis. Hitler's dismissal of atomic research was the first of his technological mistakes. The second was his concentration of resources on the development of the rocket, which Hitler proclaimed would be "the decisive weapon of the war." As the tide turned against Germany, the Nazi leadership seized upon the promise of "robot aircraft," championed by the young scientist Wernher von Braun. These giant unmanned weapons were to be launched in great number and with supposedly devastating precision against enemy cities and military positions. The Allied bombing of the rocket-research base at Peenemunde, located on the Baltic Sea, in August 1943, did not deter Hitler, who firmly believed that the showering of rockets on the enemy would reverse Germany's declining military position. Nicknamed *Vergeltungswaffen*—"weapons of revenge"—the weapons were commonly known as the V2 (rocket) and the V1 (the less sophisticated "fly-ing bomb"). After the D-Day Allied landings at Normandy, the Germans launched these weapons against London. Over the next several months, some three thousand "weapons of revenge" hit London and hundreds more were launched against Allied military positions in Western Europe.

Strategically, however, the rocket campaign was a disaster: a case of too little, too late, and with too little accuracy. General Eisenhower later remarked that had the rockets been launched against England before the Allied cross-Channel invasion at Nor-mandy, they could have seriously disrupted the operation. The rocket attacks on Allied positions caused some destruction and ca-sualties and forced the Allies to divert some of their resources to attacking the sources of the new weapons, but, overall, the V1 and V2 had negligible effect and failed to slow the Allied offensive. While some 9,000 Londoners were killed by use of these weapons, such attacks had no effect on British morale. If the English had sur-vived the German bombing of 1940–41, when the Allied position was at best precarious, there was no reason to believe they would be greatly demoralized now that victory was at hand. Likewise, the damage caused by the rockets was minimal. The total rocket ton-nage of explosives that hit London was just less than 1 percent of the tonnage of Allied bombs dropped on Germany during the same period. Finally, the V1s and V2s suffered from chronic impreci-sion; most of them failed to hit their targets.

The ultimate benefit to the Allies of Hitler's obsession with achieving a technological breakthrough in rocketry was that it di-verted limited German resources from application to more produc-tive enterprises. The V-weapons campaign was expensive. Had the funds devoted to the rockets been spent on rebuilding the air force, the Germans could have produced 24,000 more planes—which would have gone far to challenging Allied supremacy in the air.

(3) The Moral Struggle: Mobilizing Popular Will

In the essential effort of all belligerent governments to enlist the support of their peoples, the Allies had a significant advantage over the Axis, for their struggle against the Axis had a strong moral dimension. Hatred of Hitler and the determination to eradicate the Nazism that he embodied brought together the Allies and provided the essential element in convincing their armies and civilians that they were waging a "just" war. The Allies saw themselves fighting on behalf of civilization against barbarism. A Nazi victory would lead to a return to the Dark Ages; it would, an American philosopher wrote, "destroy the freedom of Europe, . . . jeopardize every noble ideal of human culture, every high concept of human morality, every fine achievement of hard-won democracy." The other Axis powers—Mussolini's crude nationalism and Japan's militarism—also embodied barbarism that helped to cement the Allied moral crusade and justify the demand for the "unconditional surrender" of the Axis. Americans, of course, held the Japanese in special contempt.

The moral element of the Allied sentiment found expression in the guiding principles embraced at the Atlantic Conference and restated in the Declaration of the United Nations. A central role for the Soviet Union in the Allied coalition could have undermined the Allied cause, for a communist dictatorship with a sorry record of persecution of political opponents hardly seemed compatible with the liberal values espoused by the democracies. The common cause of defeating Germany, however, transformed the image of the Soviet Union. British and Americans generally drew a distinction between fascism as an absolute evil and communism as a lesser one. More important, the resistance of the Russian army and people to the Germans transformed the Western image of the Soviet Union from a backward, inept, corrupt regime to that of a patriotic, progressive, and resourceful country.

Besides the hatred of Hitler as a rallying point, the moral imperative rested on the fact that the major Allies had all been victims of aggression. The British had absorbed German bombing and lost their Southeast Asian colonies, the Americans had been attacked at Pearl Harbor and had lost their possessions in the western Pacific, and the Soviets had been directly invaded by a large German army. It is axiomatic that peoples who are fighting in self-defense against an aggressor have a greater sense of righteousness than those peoples whose armies have invaded another country. Recog nizing this, Stalin presented the war to the Soviet people not as a battle between communism and fascism, but as a sacred mission. During the dark days of early 1942, he told Soviet forces: "The Red Army's strength lies above all in the fact that it is not waging a predatory, imperialist war, but a patriotic war, a war of liberation, a just war."

The struggle against Germany transformed the relationship between the Soviet government and people. Reports of the fighting and government propaganda convinced the army and the public that they had to be prepared to endure enormous sacrifices because they were part of the war to save Mother Russia. The very name by which the war was known in the Soviet Union—the Great People's Patriotic War—emphasized the continuity with the Russian past and the historic record of repelling invaders of the Motherland. Reports of German atrocities against Russian troops and civilians were a daily ingredient of Soviet propaganda, which presented the struggle as a "war of extermination" that would "annihilate to the last man all Germans." The patriotism instilled by the resistance to the Germans indeed united the peoples of the Soviet Union to a degree unknown since the Bolshevik Revolution.

On the other side, the Axis states fought with less commitment. Aggressive war was not generally popular in any of the three Axis countries, for it was the decision of dictators in Germany and Italy and of the military leadership in Japan. To be sure, in the early days of the actual fighting, government propaganda built upon the Axis success on the battlefield to generate popular enthusiasm. Support in Axis countries, however, never approximated the level of popular commitment among Allied peoples. As the war went on and turned against the Axis, their respective publics were subjected to propaganda that minimized battlefield losses and promised a reversal of military fortunes. The Allied invasion of Italy exposed such shallow popular commitment that its armed forces collapsed. In Germany and Japan, censorship and propaganda could not conceal realities indefinitely, especially after Allied bombing destroyed factories and homes. The Nazi propaganda machine denounced the Allies as tools of Jews, spoke of the "treachery of Bolshevism," and used other shopworn cliches to try to keep an increasingly disillusioned public in line. Fear that a Soviet assault on Germany would bring widespread atrocities (a staple of Nazi propaganda) helped to keep Germans fighting, but with no illusions that they would win. After the war, a young German woman recalled the attitudes of men as they prepared for the last battles: "There was nothing morbid about the way they accepted their fate, although none of them wanted to die for one man's insanity. When they left, they knew that soon . . . they would be killed, and that the war was already lost for Germany. None of them survived." In Japan, the government made desperate appeals for public support as a matter of honor, but soldiers and the public knew that the war was lost. Morale was shattered. Having been told earlier that the Americans could not ever recover from the Pearl Harbor attack, much less fight effectively in jungles, the Japanese were devastated by news of the American advance across the Pacific and reports of the enormous Japanese losses in those island battles. One Japanese pilot wrote that "It was obvious that Japan had no hope at all of regaining supremacy on the sea or in the air." The relentless American bombing and blockade brought the war home to millions of Japanese. As one Japanese civilian said later: "The government kept telling us that we would defeat the United States, but as my house was burned down and I had no food, clothing, or shelter, I did not know how I could go on."

The moral purpose of the Allied cause was, it must be noted, seriously undermined by the Soviet Union's brutal warfare against its neighbors. The Soviet Union's transformation into a major Allied partner and its prominent, and at times heroic, role in defeating Germany did not change its contempt for, and its willingness to slaughter, those "lesser peoples" of Eastern Europe. To those peoples caught between Germany and the Soviet Union—in what have been called the "bloodlands" running from present-day Poland, the Baltic states (Estonia, Latvia, Lithuania), Ukraine, Belarus, and the western edge of Russia—there was no discernible difference between the invaders from the west and those from the east. Both indulged in terrifying orgies of mass killing. Altogether some 14 million people died at the hands of the Germans and Soviets during the immediate prewar and wartime years. In his book, *Bloodlands:*

Europe between Hitler and Stalin, the historian Timothy Snyder writes that "Hitler and Stalin rose to power in Berlin and Moscow, but their visions of transformation concerned above all the lands between." Before the war, Stalin ordered the slaughter of Polish and Ukranian minorities within the Soviet Union. During the war, the peoples in this region experienced two, sometimes three, invasions and occupations by the German and Soviet armies. When Soviet armies invaded eastern Poland in 1939 (the notorious Nazi-Soviet Pact having provided for the division of Poland), Stalin ordered the execution of Polish prisoners. The most monstrous act was the Katyn massacre (named for the forest near the Soviet city of Smolensk) where in 1940 the Soviets killed some 20,000 Polish army officers. The Soviet conquest of the Baltic states (also sanctioned by the Nazi-Soviet Pact) brought with it the Soviet secret police's deportation of hundreds of thousands of political prisoners and the killing of thousands of others. Some 1 million prisoners from the "bloodlands" died in the Soviet *Gulag* and another 6 million died from the Soviet's intentional famines and killings.

When the Soviet Army gained the military initiative after the battle of Stalingrad, Stalin used it as an instrument of assuring Soviet control over its western neighbors. Again, Poland was the principal victim. In the spring of 1944, Jews in the Warsaw ghetto, supported by the Polish underground, rebelled against their German oppressors, who, with the connivance of the Soviets, brutally suppressed the Warsaw Uprising. With the Soviet Army just fifty miles away, Stalin ordered it to halt, refused to send any aid to the rebels, and denied American and British requests to airlift supplies to them. Some 15,000 insurgents and 250,000 civilians were killed as the Germans crushed the uprising and then leveled the city with a devastating bombing raid. Stalin thus allowed the Germans to eliminate thousands of Poles who might have challenged his plans to dominate postwar Poland. Snyder and fellow historian Gerhard Weinberg underscore the deceit of the Soviets. Snyder writes: "The Nazi and Soviet regimes . . . sometimes held compatible goals as foes: as when Stalin chose not to aid the rebels in Warsaw . . . thereby allowing the Germans to kill people who would later have resisted communist rule." Weinberg adds: "With both the British and American governments pressing him repeatedly, Stalin opted as he had in 1939 for an accommodation, even if tacit and temporary with Germany, if that helped accomplish the final destruction of Polish independence. If the cost was to be great damage to the alliance with his two Western partners, so be it. The priorities in Soviet policy seemed clear to Stalin." The Soviet Army's "liberation" of Eastern Europe thus was truly a "conquest." However legitimate the Soviet Union's concerns about its security, its unnecessarily brutal warfare stained the morality of the Allied cause.

(4) The Quality of Leadership: Meeting the Challenge

Wars magnify the qualities of leaders. They typically assume, or are granted, greater powers than in peacetime. They come to speak and act on behalf of the nation with rarely challenged authority. In effect, they come to embody the nation at war.

Most of the great decisions of World War II were made by its four most important leaders: Roosevelt, Stalin, Churchill, and Hitler. They were very different men in many ways: Roosevelt and Churchill were democratic leaders, while Stalin and Hitler were dictators. Roosevelt, Churchill, and Stalin had not expected that waging a war would be the ultimate test of their leadership, whereas Hitler had made war a central objective of the Nazi regime. Yet facing the test of all-out war, it was Roosevelt, Churchill, and even the ruthless Stalin who became leaders of real substance. Hitler, however, failed miserably.

Roosevelt, Churchill, and Stalin shared a number of military, diplomatic, and political attributes that contributed to the success of the Allies. Each played a major role in general strategic plans, but generally deferred to the judgment of military leaders in the implementation of strategy. Roosevelt relied on the highly respected General George C. Marshall, the army chief of staff and the "first among equals" on the Anglo-American combined chiefs of staff, whose enormously impressive organizational skills and coordination of military resources were fundamental to the Allied victory. To the annoyance of his generals, Churchill fancied himself a military genius, but while not always pleased with their plans, he always deferred to their recommendations. To meet the challenge of the Nazi invasion, Stalin reformed the Soviet Army and based appointments on merit rather than, as previously, on Communist Party status. His appointment of Marshal Georgi Zhukov as deputy supreme commander was critical to the victory at Stalingrad and the overall revival of the Red Army.

Diplomatically, Roosevelt, Churchill, and Stalin unequivocally committed their nations to Allied unity. They held firmly to the "unconditional surrender" demand and they recognized that their differences, as serious as they might be at times, were less significant than their common interest in defeating the Axis. In the process, the Big Three confounded the hopes of the Germans and the Japanese, which both held until the last days of the war, that they could exploit Allied differences. As the war ended, Marshall observed that "our greatest triumph lies in the fact that we achieved the impossible, Allied military unity of action."

Politically, Roosevelt, Churchill, and Stalin were adept at rallying their publics to support the war. They exploited the Allied advantage, as victims of aggression and saviors of the world against fascism, in presenting the struggle as a moral cause. Each used radio to communicate directly with their peoples (Churchill and Roosevelt were very effective orators) and helped develop propaganda that reached the public through films, books, pamphlets, speeches, and other forums.

On the other side, Hitler proved inept; as in other aspects of the war, a dramatic transformation in his leadership took place. During the 1930s and the triumphant early years of the war, Hitler's capacity to inspire the German people and to determine military strategy were critical to Nazi success. Once Nazi supremacy was challenged, however, Hitler's weaknesses—his fanatical belief in his infallibility, his refusal to take advice, his crude judgments of other peoples—undermined Germany's fortunes. Unlike the Allied leaders, he insisted on making all the important military decisions, interfering with commanders down to the smallest details; as a strategist, he knew only two principles: pursue the offensive; fight to the death. Time and again, his orders condemned German forces to unwise campaigns and unnecessarily heavy losses.

Hitler's incompetence as commander was compounded by his distrust of professional officers and his appointment of generals on the basis of loyalty. The most notorious and damaging example of Hitler's rewarding of incompetence was air force commander Herman Goering, who was largely responsible for the failure of the air force, but whom Hitler made, as marshal of the reich, the highest ranking officer in the armed forces. As the Allied armies moved toward Germany, Hitler was increasingly secluded and relied on the Nazi propaganda machine to cultivate the well-honed myth of his military genius, which, it was purported, would bring an eventual German victory. In the end, that image could not be sustained, as the Allies overwhelmed Germany. As he prepared to end his life, Hitler characteristically blamed others for the catastrophe that he had brought upon his nation.

No one of the above factors—industrial supremacy, transformation of the armed forces, popular support, or quality of leadership—was sufficient in itself to guarantee Allied victory. These factors were closely related and collectively go a long way toward explaining the ways in which developments behind the lines affected the battles. Still, with all of their disadvantages, the Axis nations might have reversed their fortunes, or at least prolonged the war. More astute leadership on Hitler's part could have narrowed the Allies' industrial advantage, enhanced the weaponry at Germany's disposal, reduced battlefield losses, and challenged the Americans in developing an atomic bomb. The Allies persevered, with their moral justification providing the one advantage that the Axis had no way of matching.

World War II was the most significant event of the twentieth century. It affected the lives of peoples throughout the world, brought an end to the noxious barbarism of the Axis, and enabled liberal values to prevail. With the United States and Soviet Union emerging as the two strongest powers by 1945, World War II also led to the prolonged struggle known as the Cold War. In Asia, the Middle East, and Africa, the Allied commitment to self-determination of native peoples and the reduced strength of the European colonial powers stimulated nationalism; within two decades, Western imperialism had virtually ended. By the end of the twentieth century, the values for which the Allies fought in World War II had been widely realized. The abrupt end of the Cold War and the dissolution of the Soviet Union brought democratic institutions to millions of people who had lived, some of them for their entire lives, under authoritarian rule. In the Third World, democracy also spread at the turn of the twenty-first century. In many places, the commitment to democratic institutions was fragile, but, clearly, liberal values reflected in the increased attention to human rights have increasingly become the standard by which the international community judges the actions of governments. The United Nations, an imperfect but still viable institution, has advanced the cause of human rights and has also twice been the agency of opposing acts of aggression, in Korea and the Persian Gulf, that were every bit as blatant as were those of the Germans, Japanese, and Italians that led to World War II.

Two decades after the end of World War I, fighting in Asia and Europe marked the beginning of World War II. In the nearly seven decades since the end of that war, the world has been spared another major war. The defeat of fascism and the triumph of the Allies brought in their train political and ideological changes that have led to a more stable, if not peaceful, world. The allied cause must still be judged the most necessary of wars.

Bibliographical Essay

Overview

There is a vast literature on World War II. For a general introduction several works are very useful: B. H. Liddell Hart, *History of the Second World War* (London, 1970); Gordon Wright, *The Ordeal of Total War, 1939–1945* (New York, 1968); Henri Michel, *The Second World War,* trans. Douglas Permei (2 vols., New York, 1975); Robert Leckie, *Delivered From Evil: The Saga of World War II* (New York, 1987); Martin Gilbert, *The Second World War* (New York, 1989); Michael Lyons, *World War II* (Englewood Cliffs, NJ, 1989); Peter Calvocoressi, Guy Wint, and John Pritchard, *Total War: The Story of World War II* (Rev. ed., New York, 1989); Robert A. C. Parker, *Struggle for Survival: The History of the Second World War* (Oxford, UK, 1989); H. P. Willmott, *The Great Crusade: A New Complete History of the Second World War* (London, 1989); Gerhard L. Weinberg, *A World at Arms: A Global History of World War II* (New York, 1994); David Miller, *Great Battles of World War II: Major Operations That Affected the Course of the War* (London, 1998); Joanna Bourke, *The Second World War: A People's History* (London, 2001); Williamson Murray and Allan R. Millett, *A War to*

146

Be Won: Fighting the Second World War (Cambridge, MA, 2000); Thomas W. Zeiler, *Annihilation: A Global History of World War II* (New York, 2011). Although self-serving, Winston S. Churchill, *The Second World War* (6 vols., Boston, 1948–1953), is a brilliantly written memoir and history of the war. Ian Kershaw, *Fateful Choices: Ten Decisions that Changed the World, 1940–1941* (London, 2007) is a singularly important work on the origins of the war in Europe and the Pacific.

American involvement in the war is covered in a number of valuable studies, including: Michael C. C. Adams, *The Best War Ever: America and World War II* (Baltimore, 1994); Studs Terkel, *"The Good War": An Oral History of World War II* (New York, 1984); Geoffrey Perret, *There's A War To Be Won: The United States Army in World War II* (New York, 1991); Paul Fussell, *Wartime: Understanding and Behavior in the Second World War* (New York, 1989); and D. Clayton James and Anne Sharp Wells, *From Pearl Harbor to V-J Day: The American Armed Forces in World War II* (Chicago, 1995).

Each of the American military services has published extensive histories of the war. Specific volumes relating to operations discussed in the text will be cited under the appropriate chapter headings. In *The Two Ocean War* (Boston, 1963), the official naval historian Samuel Eliot Morison provides a succinct and vivid summary of his fifteen-volume history. A valuable supplement to Morison's book is John Creswell, *Sea Warfare, 1939–1945* (Rev. ed., Berkeley, 1967), which incorporates much material on the British, Japanese, and German naval warfare. For a general introduction to the major political and strategic issues from the American perspective, two older works are still pertinent: Kent Roberts Greenfield, *American Strategy in World War II: A Reconsideration* (Baltimore, 1963) and Samuel Eliot Morison, *Strategy and Compromise* (Boston, 1958).

Chapter One

Robert A. Divine, *The Reluctant Belligerent, American Entry into World War II* (2d ed., New York, 1979) provides a detailed introduction to the issues confronting the United States from 1939 to 1941.

Arnold A. Offner, *The Origins of the Second World War, American Foreign Policy and World Politics 1917–1941* (New York, 1975) integrates the legacy of World War I and interwar policy with the American response to the international crises of the late 1930s. Justus D. Doenecke and John E. Wilz, *From Isolation to War, 1931–1941* (3d ed., Wheeling, IL, 2003), traces the hesitant and inconsistent American policy of the decade leading to Pearl Harbor. T. R. Fehrenbach, *F.D.R.'s Undeclared War* (New York, 1967) emphasizes the influence of public opinion as a hindrance to effective diplomacy. William L. Langer and S. Everett Gleason, *The Challenge to Isolation: The World Crisis of 1937–1940 and American Foreign Policy* (2 vols., New York, 1952), an early work based on original sources before they were opened to other scholars, remains the most comprehensive study of American policy of the 1937–40 period. For a highly critical perspective of the assumptions underlying American policy, see Bruce M. Russett, *No Clear and Present Danger: A Skeptical View of United States Entry into World War II* (New York, 1972). Waldo Heinrichs, *Threshold of War: Franklin D. Roosevelt and American Entry into World War II* (New York, 1988), provides a balanced appraisal of Roosevelt's leadership in the latter half of l941, noteworthy for its integration of the crises in Europe and Asia.

Scholarship on the origins of the war in Europe has tended to focus on issues of responsibility. John W. Wheeler-Bennett, *Munich: Prologue to Tragedy* (London, 1948) and Leonard Mosley, *On Borrowed Time: How World War II Began* (New York, 1969) are representative of those who blame the Western powers for their failure to recognize Germany's threat. William R. Rock, *British Appeasement in the 1930s* (London, 1977) and Martin Thomas, *Britain, France, and Appeasement: Anglo-French Relations in the Popular Front Era* (Oxford, UK, 1996) explore fully the bases of appeasement. Laurence D. Lafore, *The End of Glory: An Interpretation of the Origins of World War II* (Philadelphia, 1972) emphasizes the indecision of France and the collapse of the European international system. The major challenge to the conventional interpretation of German aggression as the basic cause of the war was offered by A. J. P. Taylor in the *Origins of the Second World War* (New York,

1972); in this revisionist account, Hitler is seen as seeking legitimate German interests; war was forced by Great Britain and France. The debate generated by Taylor's argument is summarized in Wm. Roger Louis (ed.), *The Origins of the Second World War: A. J. P. Taylor and His Critics* (New York, 1972). Among the leading critics is Alan Bullock, author of *Hitler: A Study in Tyranny* (New York, 1964); while acknowledging Hitler's abilities, Bullock sees his amoral and cynical opportunism as making war almost inevitable. Up-to-date accounts of the complex origins of the war are provided by: Philip M. H. Bell, *The Origins of the Second World War in Europe* (Rev. ed., New York, 1997); Andrew J. Crozier, *The Causes of the Second World War* (Oxford, UK, 1997); R. J. Overy, *The Origins of the Second World War* (Rev. ed., New York, 1998); and Donald C. Watt, *How War Came: The Immediate Origins of the Second World War, 1938–1939* (London, 1989).

The extent to which Nazi Germany threatened the United States is explored in three works: James V. Compton, *The Swastika and the Eagle: Hitler, The United States and the Origins of World War II* (Boston, 1967); Alton Frye, *Nazi Germany and the American Hemisphere, 1934–1941* (New Haven, CT, 1967); and Hans Trefousse, *Germany and American Neutrality, 1939–1941* (New York, 1951). The quasi-war on the Atlantic is described by Paul S. Ryan and Thomas A. Bailey in *Hitler versus Roosevelt: Undeclared Naval War* (New York, 1979).

The American response to the deterioration of European stability is traced fully by Arnold A. Offner, in *American Appeasement: United States Foreign Policy and Germany, 1933–1938* (Cambridge, MA, 1969) and by Robert A. Divine, *The Illusion of Neutrality* (Chicago, 1962). The influence of isolationism is examined by Selig Adler in *The Isolationist Impulse: Its Twentieth Century Reaction* (New York, 1957) and by Manfred Jonas in *Isolationism in America, 1935–1941* (Ithaca, 1966). Charles Chatfield, *For Peace and Justice: Pacifism in America 1914–1941* (Knoxville, TN, 1971) emphasizes the role of pacifists in promoting isolationism. Three works by Wayne S. Cole—*America First: The Battle Against Intervention, 1940–1941* (Madison, WI, 1953), *Charles A. Lindbergh and the Battle Against Intervention in World War II* (New York,

1974), and *Roosevelt and the Isolationists, 1932–1945* (Lincoln, NE, 1983)—examine judiciously the leadership, organization, objectives, and strategies of the isolationists. On the other side of the debate over foreign policy, see Mark L. Chadwin, *The War Hawks of World War II* (Chapel Hill, NC, 1968).

The emergence of the close relationship between the United States and Great Britain is detailed in: David Reynolds, *The Creation of the Anglo-American Alliance, 1937–1941: A Study in Competitive Cooperation* (Chapel Hill, NC, 1982); Joseph P. Lash in *Roosevelt and Churchill, 1939–1941: The Partnership That Saved The West* (New York, 1976); Theodore A. Wilson, *The First Summit: Roosevelt and Churchill at Placentia Bay, 1941* (Boston, 1969); Thomas Parrish, *To Keep the British Afloat: FDR's Men in Churchill's London, 1941* (New York, 2009); Norman Moss, *19 Weeks: America, Britain, and the Fateful Summer of 1940* (Boston, 2003); Warren Kimball, *The Most Unsordid Act: Lend-Lease, 1939–1941* (Baltimore, 1969); and Philip Seib, *Broadcasts from the Blitz: How Edward R. Murrow Helped Lead America Into War* (Washington, DC, 2006). Challenging the conventional interpretation of Anglo-American interest in defeating Nazism is Patrick Buchanan's *Churchill, Hitler, and "The Unnecessary War": How Britain Lost Its Empire and the West Lost the World* (New York, 2008).

The German blitzkrieg of 1940, the fall of France and the bombing campaign against Britain are covered in: Karl-Heinz Frieser and John T. Greenwood. *The Blitzkrieg Legend: The 1940 Campaign in the West* (Annapolis, MD, 2005); Ronald Powaski, *Lightening War: Blitzkrieg in the West, 1940* (Hoboken, NJ, 2003); Julian Jackson, *The Fall of France: The Nazi Invasion of 1940* (London, 2003); Robert Jackson, *Dunkirk: The British Evacuation, 1940* (London, 2002); Hugh Sebag-Montefiore, *Dunkirk: Fight to the Last Man* (Cambridge, MA, 2006); Ernest R. May, *Strange Victory: Hitler's Conquest of France* (New York, 2000); Paul Addison and Jeremy A. Crang, eds. *The Burning Blue: A New History of the Battle of Britain* (London, 2000); and Michael Korda, *With Wings Like Eagles; A History of the Battle of Britain* (New York, 2008).

The German invasion of the Soviet Union and the Anglo-American response can be traced in John Erickson and David Dilks, eds.,

Barbarossa: The Axis and the Allies (Edinburgh, UK, 1994); Steven M. Miner, *Between Churchill and Stalin: The Soviet Union, Great Britain, and the Origins of the Grand Alliance* (Chapel Hill, NC, 1988); David E. Murphy, *What Stalin Knew: The Enigma of Barbarossa* (New Haven: Yale, 2005); Raymond H. Dawson, *The Decision to Aid Russia, 1941: Foreign Policy and Domestic Politics* (Chapel Hill, NC, 1959).

For a comprehensive overview of American-Asian relations, see Akira Iriye, *Across the Pacific: An Inner History of American–East Asian Relations* (New York, 1967), which underscores the importance of misperceptions and misunderstandings. Charles E. Neu, *The Troubled Encounter: The United States and Japan* (New York, 1975), William L. Neumann, *America Encounters Japan: From Perry to MacArthur* (Baltimore, 1963), and Walter LaFeber, *The Clash: A History of U.S.-Japan Relations* (New York, 1997) place the war within the broader context of Japanese-American relations.

Japan's expansion has been explored in several studies: John V. Toland, *The Rising Sun: The Decline and Fall of the Japanese Empire, 1936–1945* (2 vols., New York, 1970), valuable principally for its reconstruction of the Japanese mentality; F. C. Jones, *Japan's New Order in East Asia: Its Rise and Fall, 1937–1945* (New York, 1954), which stresses the opportunism of Japanese imperialism; James B. Crowley, *Japan's Quest for Autonomy: National Security and Foreign Policy* (Princeton, NJ, 1966); and Michael A. Barnhart, *Japan Prepares for Total War: The Search for Economic Security, 1919–1941* (Ithaca, NY, 1987), which set forth the essential rationality of Japan's drive for East Asian hegemony. The movement toward an alliance with Germany is most fully analyzed by Ernest L. Presseisen, *Germany and Japan: A Study in Totalitarian Diplomacy, 1933–1941* (The Hague, 1958) and Frank W. Ikle, *German-Japanese Relations, 1936–1940* (New York, 1956).

The crisis in Japanese-American relations is examined most fully in Dorothy Borg and Shumpei Okamoto, eds., *Pearl Harbor as History: Japanese-American Relations, 1931–1941* (New York, 1973). A more recent and briefer collection of insightful essays is *Pearl Harbor Revisited*, ed. Robert W. Love (New York, 1995). Dorothy Borg, *The United States and the Far Eastern Crisis of 1933–1938:*

From the Manchurian Incident Through the Initial Stage of the Undeclared Sino-Japanese War (Cambridge, MA, 1964) traces the halting U.S. response to the deterioration of Asian stability. The broader story is told in Akira Iriye, *The Origins of the Second World War in Asia and the Pacific* (New York, 1987) and Haruo Tohmatsu and H. P. Willmott, *A Gathering Darkness: The Coming of War to the Far East and the Pacific, 1921–1942* (Wilmington, DE, 2004). James H. Herzog, *Closing the Open Door: American-Japanese Relations, 1936–1941* (Annapolis, MD, 1973) stresses the influence of naval developments on policy. Waldo H. Heinrich's, *American Ambassador: Joseph G. Grew and the Development of the United States Diplomatic Tradition* (Boston, 1966) analyzes the course of Japanese-American relations. A superb account of the American military position in the Pacific is provided by Brian McAllister Linn in *Guardians of Empire: The U.S. Army and the Pacific, 1902–1940* (Chapel Hill, NC, 1997). The British-American relationship with respect to Japan's expansion is examined in two works: Bradford A. Lee, *Britain and the Sino-Japanese War, 1937–1939* (Stanford, CA, 1973); and Peter Lowe, *Great Britain and the Origins of the Pacific War: A Study of British Policy in East Asia, 1937–1941* (Oxford, UK, 1977).

The events leading to the Pearl Harbor attack have been the subject of numerous studies. Herbert Feis, *The Road to Pearl Harbor: The Coming of War between the United States and Japan* (Princeton, NJ, 1950), an early account intended to address critics who charged Roosevelt with plotting war, remains valuable for its detailed presentation of American policy. Paul W. Schroeder, *The Axis Alliance and Japanese-American Relations, 1941* (Ithaca, NY, 1958), criticizes United States policy after July 1941 for its inflexibility and failure to comprehend Japan's willingness to compromise. Robert J. C. Butow, *Tojo and the Coming of War* (Princeton, NJ, 1961) analyzes Japan's policy-making process, while Nobutaka Ike, trans. and ed., *Japan's Decision for War: Records of 1941 Policy Conferences* (Stanford, CA, 1967) provides insight into the internal debate over the necessity for war. Peter Wetzler, *Hirohito and War: Imperial Tradition and Military Decision Making in Prewar Japan* (Honolulu, 1998) reexamines the conventional view of the limited role of the Emperor. Gordon

W. Prange, *At Dawn We Slept: The Untold Story of Pearl Harbor* (New York, 1981), is a dramatic, minute-by-minute reconstruction of the events of December 7, 1941. The domestic repercussions of the surprise attack are examined by Martin V. Melosi in *The Shadow of Pearl Harbor: Political Controversy over the Surprise Attack, 1941–1946* (College Station, TX, 1977). On the troublesome question of why the United States failed to anticipate the attack, the standard work remains Roberta Wohlstetter's *Pearl Harbor: Warning and Decision* (Stanford, CA, 1962).

Chapter Two

Samuel Eliot Morison, *The Rising Sun in the Pacific, 1931–April 1942* (Boston, 1948) discusses the demise of American naval power in the aftermath of the Pearl Harbor attack. John Toland, *But Not in Shame: The Six Months after Pearl Harbor* (New York, 1962) provides a vivid description of the Japanese conquests. Louis Morton, *The Fall of the Philippines* (Washington, DC, 1952) is the standard work analyzing the controversies surrounding MacArthur's decisions. D. Clayton James, *The Years of MacArthur* (3 vols., Boston, 1970–1985) is the principal biography of the American commander: judicious in his appraisal of MacArthur's career, James is highly critical of his strategy in the Philippines. William Manchester, *American Caesar: Douglas MacArthur, 1880–1964* (Boston, 1978) and Michael Schaller, *Douglas MacArthur: The Far Eastern General* (New York, 1989) are highly critical appraisals. Carol Morris Petillo, *Douglas MacArthur: The Philippine Years* (Bloomington, IN, 1981), contends that MacArthur had an emotional dependency on the Philippines that made it difficult for him to assess the military situation there objectively. William H. Bartsch *December 8, 1941: MacArthur's Pearl Harbor* (College Station, TX, 2003) examines his actions as the war began. Shortly before his death, MacArthur reflected on his career in his *Reminiscences* (New York, 1964); to the end, he defended his wartime actions and criticized the European priority of the leadership in Washington. The full dimension of the wartime tragedy of the Philippines is examined by Theodore Friend, *Between Two Empires: The Ordeal of the Philippines, 1929–1946* (New Haven, CT, 1965).

The Japanese conquests of early 1942 and their ideological implications are explored by: Christopher Bayly and Tim Harper. *Forgotten Armies: The Fall of British Asia, 1941–1945.* (Cambridge, MA,
2004); Gerald Horne, *Race War! White Supremacy and the Japanese
Attack on the British Empire* (New York, 2004): and Eri Hotta, *Pan-
Asianism and Japan's War, 1931–1945* (New York, 2007).

On the "home front," four works offer various perspectives:
John Blum, *V Was For Victory: Politics and Culture During World
War II* (New York, 1976); Richard R. Lingeman, *Don't You Know
There's A War On? The American Home Front, 1941–1945* (New
York); Richard W. Polenberg, *War and Society: The United States,
1941–1945* (Philadelphia, 1972); and Alan M. Winkler, *Home Front
U.S.A.: America during World War II* (2d ed., Wheeling, IL, 2000).
Winkler's work is the most comprehensive and up-to-date. Blend-
ing a study of Roosevelt's leadership with a portrait of life in the
wartime White House is Doris Kearns Goodwin's *No Ordinary Time:
Franklin and Eleanor Roosevelt: The Home Front in World War II*
(New York, 1994). On the ways that Americans perceived the war,
see: Jeanine Basinger, *The World War II Combat Film: Anatomy of
a Genre* (New York, 1986) and Clayton R. Koppes and Gregory D.
Black, *Hollywood Goes to War: How Politics, Profits, and Propaganda Shaped World War II Movies* (New York, 1987).

Chapter Three

Several early works trace the course of war in Europe: Sir Arthur
Bryant, *The Turn of the Tide* (New York, 1957) and *Triumph in the
West* (London, 1959); and Charles B. MacDonald, *The Mighty Endeavor: American Armed Forces in the European Theater in World
War II* (New York, 1969). More recent scholarship includes: M. K.
Dziewanowski, *War At Any Price: World War II in Europe* (Englewood Cliffs, NJ, 1991) and John Ellis, *Brute Force: Allied Strategy
and Tactics in the Second World War* (New York, 1990); Mark A.
Stoler, *Allies in War: Britain and America Against the Axis Powers,
1940–1945* (London, 2005); and Norman Davies, *No Simple Victory: World War II in Europe, 1939–1945* (New York, 2006).

The American military leaders have been the subject of solid
biographies. Forrest C. Pogue, *George C. Marshall: Vol. 2: Ordeal*

and Hope, 1939–1942 (New York, 1966) and *Vol. 3: Organizer of Victory, 1943–1944* (New York, 1973) analyze carefully the career of the U.S. Army chief of staff. Mark Stoler, *George C. Marshall: Soldier-Statesman of the American Century* (Boston, 1989) provides a thoughtful overview. Thomas Parrish, *Roosevelt and Marshall: Partners in Politics and War* (New York, 1989) grapples with two complex and very different leaders and their effective relationship. Stephen Ambrose wrote two works dealing with Eisenhower during the war: *The Supreme Commander: The War Years of Dwight D. Eisenhower* (Garden City, NY, 1969); and *Eisenhower, Vol. 1: Soldier, General of the Army, President-Elect* (New York, 1983). G. E. Patrick Murray, *Eisenhower versus Montgomery: The Continuing Debate* (Westport, CT, 1996) and A. Horne and D. Montgomery, *The Lonely Leader: Monty, 1944–1945* (London, 1994) deal with Montgomery's bitter criticism of Eisenhower. A notable and insightful effort to come to terms with Roosevelt's military leadership is the work of Eric Larrabee, *Commander in Chief: Franklin Delano Roosevelt, His Lieutenants, and Their War* (New York, 1987).

The most comprehensive surveys of the North African–Mediterranean warfare are Matthew Jones's *Britain, The United States, and the Mediterranean War, 1942–1944* (New York, 1996) and Douglas Porch's *The Path to Victory: The Mediterranean Theater in World War II* (New York, 2004), supplemented by two books by Rick Atkinson: *An Army at Dawn: The War in North Africa, 1942–1943* (New York, 2002) and *The Day of Battle: The War in Sicily and Italy, 1943–1944* (New York, 2007). Another important contribution is MacGregor Knox, *Hitler's Italian Allies: Royal Armed Forces, Fascist Regime, and the War of 1940–1943* (Cambridge, MA, 2000).

The standard critique of the Anglo-American strategy is provided in two works by Trumbull Higgins: *Winston Churchill and the Second Front* (New York, 1957); and *Soft Underbelly: The Anglo-American Controversy over the Italian Campaign* (New York, 1968). Exploring the political and military implications of the campaign are several books: Richard W. Steele, *The First Offensive, 1942: Roosevelt, Marshall and the Making of American Strategy* (Bloomington, IN, 1973); Michael Howard, *The Mediterranean Strategy in the Second World War* (New York, 1968); Arthur Funk, *The Politics of TORCH: The Allied Landings and the Algiers Putsch, 1942*

(Lawrence, KS, 1974). On the North African invasion and ensuing campaign, George F. Howe, *North Africa: Seizing the Initiative in the West* (Washington, DC, 1957) and W. G. F. Jackson, *The North African Campaign, 1940–1943* (London, 1975) are standard works. Mark Stoler, *The Politics of the Second Front: American Military Planning and Diplomacy in Coalition Warfare, 1941–1943* (Westport, CT, 1977) and Steve Weiss, *Allies in Conflict: Anglo-American Strategic Negotiations, 1938–1944* (New York, 1996) examine the Anglo-American disagreements over strategic priorities.

The German-Russian fighting can be traced in a number of works: Alan Clark, *Barbarossa: The Russian-German Conflict, 1941–1945* (New York, 1965), which is vividly written and provides a thorough analysis of Hitler's direction of the Russian campaign; Paul K. Schmidt (Paul Carell, pseud.) *Hitler Moves East* (Boston, 1965) and *Scorched Earth: The Russian-German War, 1943–1944* (Boston, 1970), which are especially valuable for presenting both sides of the combat; also good are Earl F. Zimke, *Stalingrad to Berlin: The German Defeat in the East* (Washington, DC, 1968); David M. Glantz, *The Military Strategy of the Soviet Union: A History* (London, 1992); Anthony Beevoir, *Stalingrad: The Fateful Siege, 1942–1943* (New York, 1998); Chris Bellamy, *Absolute War: Soviet Russia in the Second World War* (New York, 2007); Walter S. Dunn, Jr., *Stalin's Keys to Victory: The Rebirth of the Red Army* (Westport, CT, 2006); David M. Glantz, *Colossus Reborn: The Red Army at War, 1941–1943*. Lawrence, KS, 2005); and Marius Broekmeyer, *Stalin, the Russians, and Their War, 1941–1945* (Madison, WI, 2004).

The extensive planning for the cross-Channel invasion of France is examined by Gordon Harrison in *Cross-Channel Attack* (Washington, DC, 1951) and Forrest C. Pogue, *The Supreme Command* (Washington, DC, 1954). German preparations are detailed in Alan F. Wilt, *The Atlantic Wall, 1941–1944: Hitler's Defenses for D-Day.* (New York, 2004).

Stephen E. Ambrose, *D-Day, June 6th, 1944: The Climactic Battle of World War II* (New York, 1994) and Max Hastings, *Overlord: D-Day, June 6, 1944* (New York, 1984) capture the heroic and tragic events of that day. John Keegan, *Six Armies in Normandy: From D-Day to the Liberation of Paris* (New York, 1982) masterfully integrates the stories of the Allied and Axis armies. Carlo W. d'Este, *Decision in Normandy; The Unwritten Story of Montgomery and the Allied Campaign* (London, 1983) reexamines the landings and breakthrough within the context of Montgomery's later criticism of Eisenhower.

The role of deception is examined by W. Breuer in *Hoodwinking Hitler: The Normandy Deception* (Westport, CT, 1992) and Roger Hesketh. *Fortitude: The D-Day Deception Campaign* (Woodstock, NY, 2000). The campaign from Normandy to the defeat of Germany is chronicled in: Martin Blumenson, *Breakthrough and Pursuit* (Washington, DC, 1961); Hugh M. Cole, *The Ardennes: The Battle of the Bulge* (Washington, DC, 1965); Charles B. MacDonald, *The Last Offensive* (Washington, DC, 1973); and Oliver Wieviorka, *Normandy: The Landings to the Liberation of Paris* (Cambridge, MA, 2008). Russell Weigley, *Eisenhower's Lieutenants: The Campaigns of France and Germany, 1944–1945* (Bloomington, IN, 1981), criticizes the strategy and resource allocation of the American command.

Comprehensive and balanced treatments of the British-American air warfare, and its moral and strategic implications, include: Anthony Verrier's *The Bomber Offensive* (New York, 1968); H. S. Hansell, *The Strategic Air War Against Germany and Japan* (Washington, DC, 1986); Alan J. Levine, *The Strategic Bombing of Germany, 1940–1945* (Westport, CT, 1992); S. Garrett, *Ethics and Airpower in World II: The British Bombing of German Cities* (New York, 1990); C. C. Crane, *Bombs, Cities, and Civilians: American Airpower Strategy in World War II* (Lawrence, KS, 1993). Mark Connelly, *Reaching for the Stars: A New History of Bomber Command in World War II* (London, 2001); Marshall De Bruhl, *Firestorm: Allied Airpower and the Destruction of Dresden* (New York, 2006); Robert Ehlers, Jr. *Targeting the Third Reich: Air Intelligence and the Allied Bombing Campaigns* (Lawrence, KS, 2009); and Gian P. Gentile, *How Effective is Strategic Bombing: Lessons Learned from World War II to Kosovo* (New York, 2001).

On the naval war, Richard Snow, *A Measureless Peril: America in the Fight for the Atlantic, the Longest Battle of World War II* (New York, 2010); Arnold Hague, *The Allied Convoy System, 1939–1945: Its Organization, Defense, and Operation.* (Annapolis, MD, 2000);

and Barbara Brooks Tomblin, *With Utmost Spirit: Allied Naval Operations in the Mediterranean, 1942–1945* (Lexington, KY, 2004) each provide thorough accounts.

An important, if sometimes overstated, contribution of the British to the defeat of Germany was the work of its intelligence service in intercepting and decoding German strategic and tactical information. Since 1974, when F. W. Winterbotham in *The Ultra Secret* first revealed the British accomplishment, there have been several books on British intelligence and much controversy about their accuracy. The British government commissioned an official history: F. H. Hinsley, with E. E. Thomas, C. F. G. Ransom, and R. C. Knight, *British Intelligence in the Second World War: Its Influence on Strategy and Operations* (2 vols., London, 1984). The role of intelligence in the Battle of the Atlantic is told by David Kahn, *Seizing the Initiative: The Race to Break the German U-Boat Codes* (New York, 1998) and John Winton, *Ultra At Sea: How Breaking the Nazi Code Affected Allied Naval Strategy During World War II* (New York, 1988). The "other side" of intelligence was using it to provide "disinformation" to the enemy, a story told by Michael Howard, *Strategic Deception in the Second World War* (London, 1990).

Chapter Four

Ronald H. Spector, *Eagle Against the Sun: The American War with Japan* (New York, 1984) and John W. Dower, *War Without Mercy: Race and Power in the Pacific War* (New York, 1986) are considered the definitive works on the American-Japanese conflict. Other fine overviews are provided by Basil Collier in *The War in the Far East* (New York, 1969); Dan van der Vat in *The Pacific Campaign, World War II: The U.S.–Japanese Naval War* (London, 1992); Edwin P. Hoyt, *Japan's War: The Great Pacific Conflict* (New York, 1986); Mark D. Roehrs and William A. Renzi, *World War II in the Pacific.* (Armonk, NY, 2004); Nicholas Evan Sarantakes, *Allies Against the Rising Sun: The United States, the British Nations, and the Defeat of Imperial Japan* (Lawrence, KS, 2009); and Werner Gruhl, *Imperial Japan's World War Two, 1939–1945* (New Brunswick, NJ, 2007).

The Japanese army and its influence are recounted by: M. Harries and S. Harries, *Soldiers of the Sun: The Rise and Fall of the Imperial*

Japanese Army, 1868–1945 (London, 1991); and M. D. Kennedy, *The Military Side of Japanese Life* (Westport, CT, 1973).

The various Pacific campaigns have been studied in specialized works, including: Alan Schom, *The Eagle and the Rising Sun: The Japanese-American War, 1941–1943: Pearl Harbor through Guadalcanal* (New York, 2004); H. P. Willmott, *The War with Japan: The Period of Balance, May 1942–October 1943* (Wilmington, DE, 2002); John Miller, Jr., *Guadalcanal: The First Offensive* (Washington, DC, 1949); Gordon Prange, *Miracle at Midway* (New York, 1982); Dallas Woodbury Isom, *Midway Inquest: Why the Japanese Lost the Battle of Midway* (Bloomington, IN, 2007); Philip Crowl, *Campaign in the Marianas* (Washington, DC, 1960); Robert R. Smith, *The Approach to the Philippines* (Washington, DC, 1953); M. Hamlin Cannon, *Leyte, The Return to the Philippines* (Washington, DC, 1954); Samuel Eliot Morison, *Liberation of the Philippines* (Boston, 1959); Robert R. Smith, *Triumph in the Philippines* (Washington, DC, 1963); Harry A Gailey, *MacArthur's Victory: The War in New Guinea, 1943–1944* (New York, 2004); H. P. Willmott, *The Battle of Leyte Gulf: The Last Fleet Action* (Bloomington, IN, 2005); Harold J Goldberg. *D-Day in the Pacific: The Battle of Saipan* (Bloomington, IN, 2007); Roy Appleman, James Burns, Russell Gugeler, and John Stevens, *Okinawa: The Last Battle* (Washington, DC, 1948); Robert S. Burrell, *Ghosts of Iwo Jima* (College Station, TX, 2006); Patrick F Caruso, *Nightmare on Iwo* (Annapolis, MD, 2001); Samuel Eliot Morison, *Victory in the Pacific* (Boston, 1960); Kenneth P. Werrell, *Blankets of Fire: U.S. Bombers over Japan during World War II* (Washington, 1996); and George Feifer, *Tennozan: The Battle of Okinawa and the Atomic Bomb* (New York, 1992). On kamikaze warfare, see Hatsuho Naito, *Thunder Gods: The Kamikaze Pilots Tell Their Story* (Tokyo, 1989).

China's significance is examined in David Barrett and Larry N. Shyu, *China in the Anti-Japanese War, 1937–1945* (New York, 2001). Joseph W. Stilwell's relationship with Chiang Kai-shek has been fully described by F. Charles Romanus and Riley Sutherland in *Stilwell's Mission to China* (Washington, DC, 1953) and *Stilwell's Command Problems* (Washington, DC, 1956) and *Time Runs Out in CBI* (Washington, DC, 1959. Barbara W. Tuchman, *Stilwell and the American Experience in China, 1911–1945* (New York, 1970) uses Stilwell's career as a means of understanding Sino-American relations from the revolution of 1911 through World War II.

Chapter Five

Robert Dallek, *Franklin D. Roosevelt and American Foreign Policy, 1932–1945* (New York, 1979), is the definitive work on Roosevelt's approach to world problems. On the war years, two works by Warren Kimball examine Roosevelt's leadership in a thoughtful and balanced manner: *The Juggler: Franklin Roosevelt as Wartime Statesman* (Princeton, NJ, 1991); and *Forged in War: Roosevelt, Churchill, and the Second World War* (New York, 1997). An important overview, largely focusing on Roosevelt, is provided by Gaddis Smith, *American Diplomacy during the Second World War 1941–1945* (2d ed., New York, 1984). Two older works, while sympathetic to Roosevelt, offer some noteworthy criticisms: James MacGregor Burns, *Roosevelt: The Soldier of Freedom* (New York, 1970); and Robert A. Divine, *Roosevelt and World War II* (Baltimore, 1969). Matthew J. Dickinson, *Bitter Harvest: FDR, Presidential Power and the Growth of the Presidential Branch* (New York, 1997) carefully analyzes Roosevelt's leadership.

A number of books trace the wartime alliance with Great Britain and the Soviet Union. Early works, which tended to dwell on the deterioration of Soviet-American relations after the war, include: Herbert Feis, *Churchill, Roosevelt, Stalin: The War They Waged and the Peace They Sought* (Princeton, NJ, 1957); John L. Snell, *Illusion and Necessity: The Diplomacy of Global War, 1939–1945* (Boston, 1963); William L. Neumann, *After Victory: Churchill, Roosevelt, Stalin and the Making of the Peace* (New York, 1967); and Robert Beitzell, *An Uneasy Alliance: America, Britain, and Russia, 1941–1943* (New York, 1972). More recent contributions are: Hubert P. van Tuyll, *Feeding the Bear: American Aid to the Soviet Union, 1941–1945* (Westport, CT, 1989); Edward M. Bennett, *Franklin D. Roosevelt and the Search for Victory: American-Soviet Relations, 1939–1945* (Wilmington, DE, 1990); Amos Perlmutter, *FDR and Stalin: Not So Grand an Alliance* (Columbia, MO, 1993); David Reynolds, Warren Kimball, and A. O. Chubarian, *Allies at War: The Soviet, American, and British Experience, 1939–1945* (New York,

1994); and Bradley F. Smith, *Sharing Secrets with Stalin; How the Allies Traded Intelligence, 1941–1945* (Lawrence, KS, 1996). The most comprehensive work on the Grand Alliance remains William H. McNeill's *America, Britain and Russia: Their Cooperation and Conflict, 1941–1946* (New York, 1953). Sir Llewellyn Woodward, *British Foreign Policy in the Second World War* (5 vols., London, 1970–1976) provides a thorough overview of British policy. David Stone, *War Summits: The Meetings That Shaped World War II and the Postwar World* (Washington, DC, 2006) examines the Big Three Conferences. Much controversy surrounded the Yalta Conference. Athan Theoharis, *The Yalta Myths: An Issue in U.S. Politics, 1945–1955* (Columbia, MO, 1970) details the subsequent debate over Roosevelt's efforts to reach understandings with the Soviet Union. Diane Shaver Clemens, *Yalta* (New York, 1970) argues that Roosevelt generally acted realistically. The Potsdam Conference has been studied by Herbert Feis in *Between War and Peace: The Potsdam Conference* (Princeton, NJ, 1960) as well as by Charles L. Mee, in *Meeting at Potsdam* (New York, 1975). Robert A. Divine, *Second Chance: The Triumph of Internationalism in America during World War II* (New York, 1967) traces the activities of various groups to promote public support for the United Nations. Thomas M. Campbell, *Masquerade Peace: America's UN Policy, 1944–1945* (Tallahassee, FL, 1973) relates American efforts at fostering democratic values to an open economic system through the United Nations.

America's wartime relationship with the Soviet Union has been of special concern to historians. Representative of the 1960s New Left criticism of American diplomacy is the work of Gabriel Kolko, particularly *The Politics of War: The World and United States Foreign Policy, 1943–1945* (New York, 1968), which blames the United States for the deterioration of relations with the Soviet Union. In a less ideologically based critique of American policy, Lynn Etheridge Davis, *The Cold War Begins: Soviet American Conflict Over Eastern Europe* (Princeton, NJ, 1974) argues the American objective of the extension of the principles of the Atlantic Charter into Eastern Europe was unrealistic, failing to consider Soviet security interests. In response to Cold War revisionists, John Lewis Gaddis, in *The United States and the Origins of the Cold War* (New York, 1972), acknowledges that some of Roosevelt's policies caused problems with the Russians, but he sees the Cold War resulting principally from actions of the Soviet Union. Another balanced analysis is that of Martin F. Herz, *The Beginnings of the Cold War* (Bloomington, IN, 1966). In *Aid to Russia, 1941–1946: Strategy, Diplomacy, and the Origins of the Cold War* (New York, 1973), George C. Herring, Jr., observes how Roosevelt provided assistance as a means of assuring Stalin of Allied friendliness and support. Ralph B. Levering, *American Opinion and the Russian Alliance, 1939–1945* (Chapel Hill, NC, 1976), details the sources of American sympathy with and friendship toward the Soviet Union.

To understand the Soviet perspective on the alliance, the most complete statement is provided by Vojtech Mastny in *Russia's Road to the Cold War: Diplomacy, Warfare and the Politics of Communism, 1941–1945* (New York, 1979). Stalin's objectives, personality, and the influence of communist ideology and Russian interests on his actions are explored in two biographies: Isaac Deutscher, *Stalin: A Political Biography* (2d ed., New York, 1966); and Adam B. Ulam, *Stalin: The Man and His Era* (New York, 1973). A rare firsthand glimpse of Stalin is provided by Milovan Djilas in *Conversations With Stalin* (New York, 1962). George F. Kennan, *Russia and the West under Lenin and Stalin* (Boston, 1960) and Adam B. Ulam, *Expansion and Coexistence: Soviet-Foreign Policy, 1917–1973* (2d. ed., New York, 1974) place the wartime relationship within the context of historic Soviet objectives.

The American policy in wartime China has been most fully explored by Michael Schaller in *The U.S. Crusade in China, 1938–1945* (New York, 1979). Warren I. Cohen, *America's Response to China* (2d ed., New York, 1981) examines judiciously the history of Sino-American relations. Tang Tsou, *The American Failure in China, 1941–1950* (2 vols., Chicago, 1963) argues that the United States inadequately supported its objective of making China a great power.

Akira Iriye, *Power and Culture; The Japanese-American War, 1941–1945* (Cambridge, MA, 1981) reinterprets the Pacific war, arguing that both Japanese and American officials anticipated a return to the economic and political cooperation that had characterized Japanese-American relations in the 1920s.

The American effort to modify the colonial system, and its impact on Anglo-American relations, is the subject of several books: Wm. Roger Louis, *Imperialism at Bay: The United States and the Decolonization of the British Empire, 1941–1945* (New York, 1978); Christopher Thorne, *Allies of a Kind; The United States, Britain, and the War against Japan, 1941–1945* (New York, 1978); John J. Sbrega, *Anglo-American Relations and Colonialism in East Asia, 1941–1945* (New York, 1983); Gary R. Hess, *America Encounters India, 1941–1947* (Baltimore, 1971); and *The United States' Emergence as a Southeast Asian Power, 1940–1950* (New York, 1987). On Churchill's imperial policy, Madhusree Mukerjee, *Churchill's Secret War: The British Empire and the Ravaging of India During World War II* (New York, 2010) is an important work.

Chapter Six

On the end of the war in Europe, see: Edward G Miller, *Nothing Less than Full Victory: Americans at War in Europe 1944–1945.* Annapolis, MD, 2007) and Anthony Beevor, *Berlin: The Downfall, 1945* (London, 2004). Regarding the moral issues raised at the war's end, Michael Bess, *Choices Under Fire: Moral Dimensions of World War II* (New York, 2006) is insightful.

On the Holocaust, Lucy S. Dawidowicz, *The War Against the Jews, 1933–1945* (New York, 1975) and Saul Friedlander, *The Years of Extermination: Nazi Germany and the Jews, 1939–1945* (New York, 2007) are thorough studies. On the response of the United States to the suffering of Europe's Jews, Henry L. Feingold, *The Politics of Rescue: The Roosevelt Administration and the Holocaust* (New Brunswick, NJ, 1970), and Arthur D. Morse, *While Six Million Died: A Chronicle of American Apathy* (New York, 1968), both stress the apathy and indifference of American officials. Robert Abzug, *Inside the Vicious Heart: Americans and the Liberation of the Nazi Concentration Camps* (New York, 1985) recounts the impact of the uncovering of the death camps. The definitive works on U.S. policy are those of David S. Wyman, *In Paper Walls: America and the Refugee Crisis, 1938–1941* (Amherst, MA, 1968) and *The Abandonment of the Jews: America and the Holocaust, 1941–1945* (New York, 1984). His findings are reinforced by Joseph Bendersky,

The 'Jewish Threat': Anti-Semitic Politics of the U.S. Army (New York, 2000). Criticisms of American policy by Feingold, Morse, Wyman, and Bendersky are challenged by W. D. Rubinstein, *The Myth of Rescue: Why the Democracies Could Not Have Saved More Jews From the Nazis* (New York, 1997). For the debate on bombing the concentration camps, see: Michael J. Neufield and Michael Berenbaum, eds. *The Bombing of Auschwitz: Should the Allies Have Attempted It?* (New York, 2000).

On the end of the war in the Pacific, see: Leon V. Sigal in *Fighting to a Finish: The Politics of War Termination in the United States and Japan, 1945* (Ithaca, NY, 1988); Robert J. C. Butow, *Japan's Decision to Surrender* (Stanford, CA, 1954); Richard B. Frank, *Downfall: The End of the Imperial Japanese Empire* (New York, 1999); Thomas W. Zeiler, *Unconditional Defeat: Japan, America, and the End of World War II* (Wilmington, DE, 2004); Tsuyoshi Hasegawa, *Racing the Enemy: Stalin, Truman, and the Surrender of Japan* (Cambridge, MA, 2005); Max Hastings, *Retribution: The Battle for Japan, 1944–45* (New York, 2007).

On the development of the atomic bomb, R. G. Hewlett and O. E. Anderson, Jr., *The New World 1939–1946* (University Park, PA, 1962) is the official history of the development of the bomb. Richard Rhodes, *The Making of the Atomic Bomb* (New York, 1987) is now the standard account. Criticisms of the bomb's use began with P. M. S. Blackett, *Fear, War and the Bomb: Military and Political Consequences of Atomic Energy* (New York, 1949) and continued in other important works: Gar Alperovitz, *Atomic Diplomacy: Hiroshima and Potsdam* (New York, 1967); Martin J. Sherwin, *A World Destroyed: The Atomic Bomb and the Grand Alliance* (New York, 1975); McGeorge Bundy, *Danger and Survival: Choices About the Bomb in the First Fifty Years* (New York, 1988).

Defending the use of the bomb are: Herbert Feis, *Japan Subdued: The Atomic Bomb and the End of the War in the Pacific* (Princeton, NJ, 1961); Len Giovannitti and Fred Freed, *The Decision to Drop the Bomb* (New York, 1965); and Walter S. Shoenberger, *Decision of Destiny* (Athens, OH, 1969), which traces the development of the bomb and sees its use in 1945 as inherent in the project.

On the morality of conventional bombing, both A. C. Grayling, *Among the Dead Cities: The History and Moral Legacy of the WWII*

Bombing of Civilians in Germany and Japan (New York, 2006) and Hermann Knell, *To Destroy a City: Strategic Bombing and its Human Consequences in World War II* (Cambridge, MA, 2003) are valuable.

Conclusion

R. J. Overy, *Why the Allies Won* (New York, 1995) is the most comprehensive analysis of the reasons for the war's outcome. Also valuable are: Andrew Roberts, *Masters and Commanders: How Four Titans Won the War in the West* (New York, 2009); Stephen E. Ambrose, *The Good Fight: How World War II Was Won* (New York, 2001); and Paul Koistinen, *Arsenal of World War II: Political Economy of American Warfare, 1940–1945* (Lawrence, KS, 2004).

Important in understanding Japan's weakness are: Edward J. Drea, *Japan's Imperial Army; Its Rise and Fall, 1853–1945* (Lawrence, KS, 2009) and Walter E. Grunden, *Secret Weapons and World War II: Japan in the Shadow of Big Science* (Lawrence, KS, 2005).

On Hitler's leadership and developments in wartime Germany, see: Alan Bullock, *Hitler and Stalin: Parallel Lives* (London, 1991); John Keegan, *The Mask of Command* (New York, 1987); Earl R. Beck, *Under the Bombs: The German Home Front 1942–1945* (Lexington, KY, 1986); R. J. Overy, *War and Economy in the Third Reich* (Oxford, UK, 1994); T. Powers, *Heisenberg's War: The Secret History of the German Bomb* (New York, 1993); Richard L. Di Nardo, *Germany and the Axis Powers: From Coalition to Collapse* (Lawrence, KS, 2005); Richard J. Evans, *The Third Reich at War* (New York: 2009); Omer Bartov, *Hitler's Army: Soldiers, Nazis, and War in the Third Reich* (New York, 1999); and Adam Tooze, *The Wages of Destruction: The Making and Breaking of the Nazi Economy* (New York, 2007).

On the Soviet Union, see: John Barber and Mark Harrison, *The Soviet Home Front 1941–1945* (London, 1991); Carol Garrard and John Garrard, eds., *World War II and the Soviet People* (New York, 1993); and Geoffrey Roberts, *Stalin's Wars: From World War to Cold War, 1939–1953* (New Haven, CT, 2006). Timothy Snyder,

Bloodlands: Europe between Hitler and Stalin (New York, 2010) details German and Russian warfare on the peoples of Eastern Europe.

On Churchill's leadership and Britain during the war, see: Carlo D'Este, *Warlord: The Life of Winston Churchill at War, 1874–1945* (New York, 2008); Raymond Callahan, *Churchill and His Generals* (Lawrence, KS, 2007); Robert MacKay, *Half the Battle: Civilian Morale in Britain during the Second World War* (Manchester, UK, 2002); Richard Toye, *Churchill's Empire: The World that Made Him and the World He Made* (New York, 2010); and Max Hastings, *Winston's War: Churchill, 1940–1945* (New York, 2010).

INDEX

Algeria, 41–43
Allied Coalition, 19, 38, 87–88
  air warfare against Germany,
    51–53, 121
  air warfare against Japan, 66,
    77–79, 84, 114–17
  ground warfare against Axis in
    Europe. *See* Germany, Losses
    1942–1945
  ground warfare against Japan.
    See Japan, Defeats 1942–45
  industrial supremacy of, 129–32
  leadership of, 142–44
  modernization of armed forces,
    132–37
  moral issues and, xii–xiii,
    43–44, 104–05, 110–14,
    117–25, 140–42
  morale of its peoples, 137–42
  naval warfare against Germany.
    See Atlantic: Battle of
  strategic issues, 38–41, 51–52
  warfare against Japan. *See*
    Japan, Defeats 1942–1945
Alperovitz, Gar, 122

Atlantic, Battle of the, 7–8, 20–21,
  49–51
Atlantic Charter, 7–8, 19, 87, 95,
  138
Atomic Bomb
  development of, 114, 123–24
  questions regarding usc, 117–25
  use against Japan, 114–17
Australia, 29, 66, 69, 128
Axis Alliance, 2, 11, 59
  industrial limitations of, 129–32
  leadership of, 143–44. *See also*
    Hitler, Adolph
  morale of its peoples, 139–40
  technological shortcomings of,
    135–37

Baldwin, Hanson, 116–17
Banzai, 76, 84
Bataan Death March, 29–31, 62,
  116
Belgium, 4, 57, 132
Bendersky, Joseph, 114
Braun, Wernher von, 136
Bretton Woods Conference, 92

The United States at War: 1941–1945, Third Edition
Developmental editor: Andrew J. Davidson
Copy editor: Andrew J. Davidson
Production editor: Linda Gaio
Proofreader: Claudia Siler
Printer: Versa Press, Inc.